Mastering Scrum

GENEVIEVE COX & TUNDE ALABI

Table of Contents:

Table of Contents: 3

The Agile Fairytale 5

Scrum 11

Agile Methods: 21

Value: 33

Scrum ceremonies: 43

Epics, User Stories, Tasks 47

Acceptance Criteria, Definition of Ready and Definition of Done 51

Story pointing and slicing 55

Tools and processes 59

Roles: a deep dive 63

Scrum Master as Coach 67

Scrum Master as Mentor 73

Scrum Master as Teacher 79

Scrum Master as Manager 83

Scrum Master as Impediment Remover 87

Scrum Master as Facilitator 89

Scrum Master as Change Agent 97

Scrum Master as Servant Leader 105

Additional Content: Agile Acronyms 113

Mastering Scrum: a Conclusion 117

The Agile Fairytale

There are ways of working, and then there are Agile ways of working.

Once upon a time, there was Waterfall and that was a good way of working. In the realm of projects we worked in waterfalls. And that worked well in a world marked by predictability and stability. But suddenly, this world started to change, at a rate and pace that most businesses could not keep up with. Technology played a big part in this and over time it became clear that the projects were failing. It wasn't long before the problems of incomplete and failed projects began to emerge in their fullness. Projects weren't being completed on time, costs were expended, budgets expanded and time increased. The Waterfall way of working was no longer working in this new world.

And so it was: the search for new ways of working began. Ways of working that would cut the cost of software developments and produce better software in the process. Ways of working that embraced the ever-changing, less predictable world. And then, in 2000, came a community of software engineers who were also pioneers in the ways of working. They worked together to find a new way of working, a way of working that would enable them to deliver value, at speed, without waste or delay. They created this new way of working and they called it Agile.

They developed twelve principles and four values of Agile software development, which are now collectively known as the Agile Manifesto.

It had these four values, which privileged the things on the left *over* the things on the right:

The four Agile values:

Individuals and interactions over processes and tools

Working software over comprehensive documentation

Customer collaboration over contract negotiation

Responding to change over following a plan.

It also had these twelve principles, which offered a guide to the execution of Agile practices:

The twelve Agile principles:

1 - Our highest priority is to satisfy the customer through early and continuous delivery of valuable software.

2 - Welcome changing requirements, even late in development. Agile processes harness change for the customer's competitive advantage.

3 - Deliver working software frequently, from a couple of weeks to a couple of months, with a preference to the shorter timescale.

4 - Business people and developers must work together daily throughout the project.

5 - Build projects around motivated individuals. Give them the environment and support they need, and trust them to get the job done.

6 - The most efficient and effective method of conveying information to and within a development team is face-to-face conversation.

7 - Working software is the primary measure of progress.

8 - Agile processes promote sustainable development. The sponsors, developers, and users should be able to maintain a constant pace indefinitely.

9 - Continuous attention to technical excellence and good design enhances agility.

10 - Simplicity—the art of maximising the amount of work not done—is essential.

11 - The best architectures, requirements, and designs emerge from self-organising teams.

12 - At regular intervals, the team reflects on how to become more effective, then tunes and adjusts its behaviour accordingly.

From <*https://www.agilealliance.org/agile101/12-principles-behind-the-agile-manifesto/*>

The Agile Manifesto was circulated and, over time, it became clear that the success of Agile was clear. Data began to show that Agile projects were two times more likely to be successful and ⅓ less likely to fail than traditional Waterfall projects[1]. This is because they were more focussed on outcomes that delivered value. Furthermore, Agile had additional benefits of increased collaboration (54%); increased level of software quality (52%); increased customer satisfaction (49%); shortened time to market (43%) and reduced cost of development (42%).[2] The benefits of Agile stacked up.

And then it went mainstream!

In essence, Agile became a way of thinking that allowed us to deliver valuable results at speed, whilst meeting the

---

[1] https://standishgroup.com/, 2018
[2] https://techbeacon.com/sites/default/files/gated_asset/agile-projects-are-more-successful-than-hybrid-projects.pdf

expectations of the customer, without delay and without waste.

But the essence of this way of working wasn't completely new. In 1620, Francis Bacon articulated what he called the "New method", essentially a scientific approach to reasoning which we would align to the concept of empiricism today. Similar to Bacon's approach of reasoning, many hundreds of years later, Walter Shewhart of Bell Labs began applying a "Plan-Do-Study-Act" cycle to improve his processes and products. Just like Bacon, he used empiricism to come to rational solutions and decisions. Shewhart furthered this to result in continuous improvement.

Continuous improvement, or Kaizen, became a key element in the new production method born in Japan in the 1950s: Lean Manufacturing, or The Toyota Way. This focused on reducing what became known as the 7 core wastes of products and processes, focusing on value and value streams (the route to get to value), and finding "a way to do more and more with less and less" (Womack and Jones). Lean's Six Sigma, a set of techniques and tools for process improvement, was formed around 30 years later in 1986 by American engineer at Motorola, Bill Smith.

Around the same time as Smith, a paper appeared in the Harvard Business Review, titled "The New New Product Development Game", where the term "Scrum" was seen for the first time. Takeuchi and Ikujiro Nonaka's paper took a "rugby approach" to teamwork: "where a team tries to go the whole distance as a unit, passing the ball back and forth". Ken Schwaber used this "rugby approach" in the early 1990s at his company in a way that evolved to become "Scrum". He worked with Jeff Sutherland, who had been doing similar, to combine and formulate their ideas into a single joint paper, released in 1995, which acted as the foundations for (the later-titled) 'The Manifesto for Agile Software Development'.

All of this happened well before Agile, and many of the 'Agile' principles and approaches were being done way before Agile was born, just done independently and without recourse to the overriding objective of customer satisfaction. Agile just combined these ways of thinking, focussing on speed, value, waste, and delay. It is an ensemble of different ways of working that enable valuable delivery at speed, without waste and delay. Scrum, one of the methodologies used to do it, was born.

Scrum

Where does Scrum fit into all this?

As we saw earlier, a "rugby approach" to teamwork had already been mentioned by Takeuchi and Ikujiro Nonaka who discussed how teams in rugby worked well together, as a "team [that] tries to go the whole distance as a unit, passing the ball back and forth". Ken Schwaber used this "rugby approach" in the early 1990s at his company in a way that evolved to become "Scrum". In 1995, Ken Schwaber worked with Jeff Sutherland and, together, they created the Scrum theory. They first elucidated it in the Scrum Guide, a guide which outlines the key concept, roles, ceremonies and approach to simplifying complex problems, delivering value increments iteratively. From 2002, use of Scrum spread worldwide and Scrum became known as "a lightweight, *iterative*, and *incremental* framework for developing, delivering, and sustaining complex products.[11][12]". It was based on Empiricism:

Pillars of Scrum Empiricism:

*Empirical working means working in a fact-based, experience-based, and evidence-based manner.

From <*https://www.Scrum.org/resources/blog/three-pillars-empiricism-Scrum*>

Like three magic wishes that could come from a genie's lamp, Empiricism is based on three core principles: transparency, inspection and adaptation. These are the pillars that hold the Agile house together.

- **Transparency** - presenting and sharing the facts to enable empirical working.
- **Inspection** - explorative scrutiny and evaluation of products, processes, people and practices, done by

everyone on the Scrum team, to understand areas for improvement.

- **Adaptation** - the ability to embrace a change to enable continuous improvement.

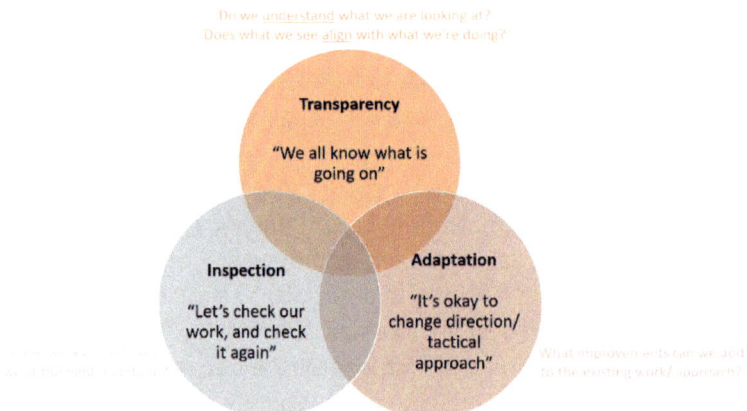

Transparency, or openness, about what is happening, helps us to see what everyone else is doing. This fosters understanding about the work being done, the state of progress, and the work needed from the rest of the team to support. Openness allows us to have positive working relationships, teamwork and the collaboration required to deliver value, at speed, without delay or waste. As Denise Morisson says: "The single most important ingredient in the recipe for success is transparency because transparency builds trust".

Example - A child wants to eat all of their Easter eggs however their mum says that they can only have one. But the child is naughty and decides to disobey their mum and eats all of their Easter eggs. Later, they feel very sick and their mum is so worried because she can't understand why they are sick so she gives them medicine which just makes the sickness worse. If the child had been open and honest about the fact that they had eaten all their chocolates, their mum would have been more helpful in being able to make their child feel better, give them the right medicine, and reassure them that they would feel well again soon.

Inspection is the intense scrutiny and evaluation of something - a piece of work, a place or a process - through total transparency and visibility, we can enable and encourage assessment and interrogation to consequently advocate change/ improvement. All the way back in 1620, Bacon was advocating the notion of rational thinking, part of which was the inspection of existing knowledge and understanding, which then encouraged adaptation of current ways of thinking/ working to improve the outcome of thought/ action. Through self-inspection, we learn more about improvement and can achieve a depth of understanding far more and far deeper than external/ outside interrogation and assessment.

Example - a bride-to-be wants to have a perfect, fairytale wedding. She sends out her friends to visit several different wedding locations - a castle, an old manor house, a beach-front restaurant, and a converted abbey. Each friend comes back with their recommendations and views, following their location visit and assessment of the various places that they went to see. The bride has all the information that she needs to make an informed decision about her wedding venue and can adjust her wedding plans accordingly. However; the inspection done by her friends is limited to their viewpoints, subject to their biases, and far less meaningful and informative than if the bride had done her own visits and formed evaluative judgements of her wedding location. Here, we can see how assessments can be informative and supportive of making decisions and/or paving the way for improvements; simultaneously can we understand the value of doing self-assessment, particularly when there is more investment in the outcome.

Adaptation is similar and yet very different from adaptation; it is the process of changing or updating something to make it better or more functional in a different setting. Adaptation, however, is when something has been changed by its environment. Adaptation is distinct in its proactive approach to change to enable improvement and effective transformation. In the Waterfall world, we failed to (inspect and) adapt as we went along, refusing to make changes - even when we saw the plan was failing. Instead we just followed the project plan blindly. In the Waterfall world this worked, originally, because change was only incremental. But in the world today, where change is the only constant, regular inspection and taking stock of things is essential. But inspection - particularly if we note change - is futile without mirrored action. And so adaptation comes into play as we adapt to the change which we have observed during the inspection of our work, processes, environment, and people.

Example - A child is making a sandcastle. They fill up the bucket with sand at the top of the beach and then walk over down to the bottom of the beach (to the spot where they are building their sandcastle) to turn the bucket over and make a turret for their sandcastle. Every time they fill up the bucket with sand and walk down the beach. But, every time, by the time they have arrived at their sandcastle spot, half of the sand has fallen out of the bucket. And so it takes them longer to build their sandcastle - twice as long as each time the buckets are only half full. However, after a few times of filling up their bucket, they realise their error and change their approach, filling up their bucket with sand next to the site of their castle. All of a sudden, their building speeds up and they complete the sand castle in time for a well-earned ice cream!

So now we see the purpose of transparency, inspection and adaptation. However, to do all these three things effectively, shared values and understanding needed to be in place. We can't inspect without respect for one another, otherwise faults may be perceived as criticisms; we can't adapt without the courage to change the course of our well-planned path. And so the Scrum values were born.

*

Fundamental to the Empirical way of thinking are the five values of Scrum, the five values which enable Empiricism to flourish:

The Scrum Values

Outlined by Sutherland and Schwaber, Scrum has five essential values which all members of the Scrum team, including the Scrum master and the product owner, must uphold. It is the responsibility of the Scrum master to not only educate the team on these values but also to ensure that these are upheld and used to guide the behaviours and attitudes of the Scrum team. These five core values are easily memorised in the acronym "FORCC": Focus, Openness, Respect, Commitment and Courage. Let's look at what each of these mean, with an example to elaborate:

Focus - the Scrum team has a shared focus: the sprint goal and the work of the sprint. This drives their work and decisions around what work to complete over the course of the sprint.

Example - A lion is hungry, its belly rumbling and its mind set on finding food as quickly as possible. All that consumes the lion is the pangs of hunger. It knows that it cannot catch its prey unless it gets within a range of 300 yards of its target. When the target is locked and within 300 yards, the lion knows his food is within easy reach. Its focus is singular and crystal clear. It crouches down, ready to focus: accelerating towards the animal before the animal sees it move. It pounces. The prey is his.

*

Openness - openness drives the attitudes and actions of the Scrum team as they are transparent about both the successes and the challenges of the work and its progress. Openness is the willingness to have an honest conversation, speaking the truth about an issue. Transparency is total visibility of all the elements involved; and vulnerability is the ability to do all this, even when the situation may be emotionally difficult or negative.

Example - A friend with relationship problems is jealous of your positive relationship with your partner and honestly confesses that she is struggling in her own relationship and is jealous of the good relationship that you and your partner have. She points out that her partner is unwilling to address the issues in their relationship - this is transparency. Furthermore, the partner is unwilling to sit down and have a heart-to-heart to address the issues - this is a lack of honesty. In the absence of honesty and transparency, the relationship breaks down: this is the same as in the work that we do!

*

Respect - all members of the Scrum team respect each other, their product owner, Scrum master, stakeholders and customer. They understand each other to be independent, capable and competent individuals.

Example - Elephants live in tightly-bonded female-led herds. They respect each other to be independently capable and yet, when a new calf is born, they come together to care for the new baby elephant. They are able to raise their offspring as individuals yet choose to raise it as a herd, working together whilst respecting each other as confident and capable individuals.

*

Commitment – everyone on the Scrum team commits, individually and as a team, to the delivery of both the sprint goal and the product goal. It is a choice to continue, regardless. It gets rid of any excuses, because you continue regardless. Circumstance, situation or external elements and variables don't deter you. A change to a commitment must always be discussed and accepted by everyone else who is bound to the commitment.

Example – A young child has a dream to study English at

Cambridge University. Throughout her SATs, her GCSEs, her AS and A Level exams, she is determined to achieve her dream of completing an English degree at Cambridge. She gets into Cambridge, goes through years of studying for her undergraduate degree. A month before her finals, however, she has appendicitis and ends up in emergency surgery. In spite of spending weeks in hospital, she continues through and does sit her final exams, gaining the degree which she committed to so long ago. Regardless of the road blockers, challenges, and obstacles, she continued, regardless, committed to her goal no matter what stood in her way.

*

Courage - like knights in shining armour, all members of the Scrum team undertake commitment to openness to point out and have the difficult conversations that otherwise lead to difficulty and trouble. They have the courage to be open about challenges and to continue to work on overcoming problems and issues that they (may) face. They willingly face up to danger, for the right cause/ reasons. Courage is bringing the elephant into the room to light.

Example - A young boy at school is seeing his classmate being bullied and hit. It takes physical courage to stand up for his classmate, facing the potential of being hit and harmed too; it also takes moral courage to stand up for what is right and to act in accordance with his conscience which tells him that bullying is wrong; and it takes emotional strength to express his anguish at seeing his classmate being picked-upon.

All of these values are ultimately inextricably interlinked and combined: you cannot have commitment to continue in the face of obstacles and difficulty without courage; you cannot have courage unless you are able to be open and identify difficulties before facing them; you cannot have openness without respect for those around you, and a willingness to be vulnerable with them in total transparency; and you cannot have focus without a sense of commitment supporting that achieving that focus. They each fuel and support one another, acting together to drive towards true value.

*

Just as any framework requires physical structuring, the Scrum framework was created around three key roles; four guiding events; and three key artefacts:

Three key roles:

- A Product Owner, a Scrum Master and Scrum Team Members (Developers) form a Scrum team. This team works together, each with different responsibilities and accountabilities, to deliver value.

Four guiding events:

- The sprint has four key events: sprint planning, daily stand-up(s) (an event which recurs on a daily basis), a sprint review and a sprint retrospective.

Three key artefacts:

- There are three key artefacts: the sprint backlog, the product backlog and the product increment, released each sprint.

And then the outlier: Backlog Refinement

- Not an event, but a continuous activity that drives continuous improvement.

- Should happen on a consistent basis to effect change in the Agile environment.

SCRUM FRAMEWORK

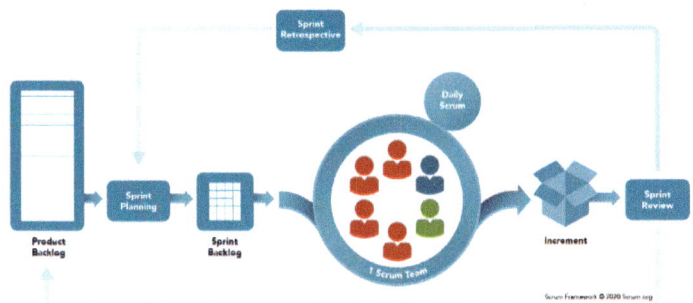

To put it in the words of the original Scrum Guide, as published by Sutherland and Schwaber, the definition of Scrum and its processes is, fundamentally and essentially simple:

Scrum is a lightweight framework that helps people, teams and organisations generate value through adaptive solutions for complex problems.

In a nutshell, Scrum requires a Scrum Master to foster an environment where:

1. A Product Owner orders the work for a complex problem into a Product Backlog.

2. The Scrum Team turns a selection of the work into an Increment of value during a Sprint.

3. The Scrum Team and its stakeholders inspect the results and adjust for the next Sprint.

4. Repeat.

From <https://Scrumguides.org/Scrum-guide.html>

Scrum created these fundamentals: Empirical thinking and its three essential pillars; the five values of Scrum; and the structured roles, events and artefacts. And so it was able to focus on customer satisfaction as the highest priority; welcoming change, from feedback cycles and continuous improvement; incremental and iterative delivery through collaboration of motivated individuals; face-to-face conversations and attention to detail whilst ensuring simplicity.

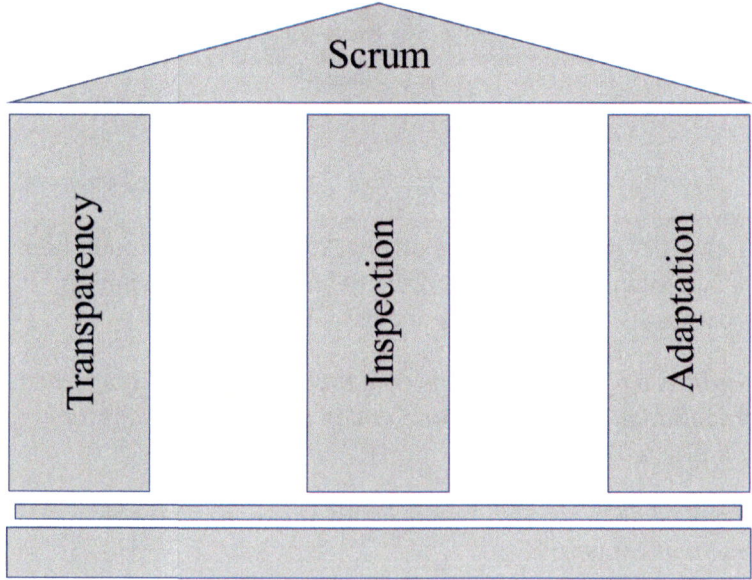

Agile Methods:

Everyone has their own approach to how they work, and everyone has their own approach to how they "Scrum".

With their origins in the Agile Manifesto, multiple methods of applying Agile ways of working have emerged, each with their own nuances and personalisations, as demanded by the environment of their implementation and/or the people using them. The most commonly recognised forms of these are: Scrum, Kanban, Scrumban, and XP. And from these, Scrum is the most popular and commonly used with approximately 87% of teams using Scrum[3]. Let's take a look at Scrum...

Scrum - according to the 2020 Scrum Guide,

"Scrum requires a Scrum Master to foster an environment where:

1. *A Product Owner orders the work for a complex problem into a Product Backlog.*

2. *The Scrum Team turns a selection of the work into an Increment of value during a Sprint.*

3. *The Scrum Team and its stakeholders inspect the results and adjust for the next Sprint.*

4. *Repeat."*

From <*https://Scrumguides.org/Scrum-guide.html*>

Essentially, in Scrum we have a Scrum team consisting of a Scrum Master, Product Owner and developers. The Product Owner determines the work to be done by the team, orders it by priority and feasibility in a backlog of items to be worked on. The developers then take these items of work and turn them

---

[3] https://stateofagile.com/

into increments of value during fixed periods of time (i.e. two weeks) called a Sprint. At the end of each Sprint, the work completed is reviewed, discussed and adjusted to enable improvements for the next Sprint.

However, there are alternatives to Scrum, and Kanban provides another popular Agile way of working which is more suited for teams that can't plan as efficiently and need to take on more ad hoc tasks.

Kanban - accordingly to Kanbanize,

"Kanban is a popular Lean workflow management method for defining, managing, and improving services that deliver knowledge work. It helps you visualise work, maximise efficiency, and improve continuously. Work is represented on Kanban boards, allowing you to optimise work delivery across multiple teams and handle even the most complex projects in a single environment.

From <https://kanbanize.com/kanban-resources/getting-started/what-is-kanban> "

Essentially, Kanban orients around a single Kanban "board" where there are columns depicting statuses of work in flow: from "To Do", "Doing/ In Progress", to "Done". There may also be a few additional columns to show where work is "In Review" or "Blocked", but the bare bones of the board would consist of those three simple headings, from left to right. Work then enters the board on an ongoing basis, firstly placed in the "To Do" column before being picked up by a developer and progressed through "Doing" to "Done". It is a continuous process of delivery where work in progress (WIP) is limited to an agreed number of tasks by the team to ensure continuous flow and prevention of taking on too many tasks which then cannot be progressed.

From the combination of Kanban and Scrum came the birth of

Scrumban...

Scrumban - a mixture of Scrum and Kanban where, due to the environment, some planning and creation of a backlog is done, however there is the additional use of the Kanban board and principles of creating and picking up tasks on an ongoing basis, without pre-planning.

Finally there is XP (Extreme Programming). This was one of the early favourites in Agile ways of working and was there right at the start of the founding of Agile, in 1996 when it was created by Kent Beck.

XP - according to EDUCBA,

"Extreme Programming (XP) has "customer satisfaction" at the heart of its framework and "teamwork" as the muscle power. Collaboration is a must for extreme programming (XP) to be successful as it takes iterative steps toward producing software for clients/customers. It is not focused on delivering the entire belt but looks at whether the needs of the client are fulfilled at every stage along the way.

From <https://www.educba.com/extreme-programming-xp-nutshell/> "

Essentially, XP focuses on delivering customer satisfaction through teamwork and bases itself on five core values to enable its delivery of fulfilling the customer expectation: communication, courage, feedback, respect and simplicity. Planning is done with respect to three key timeframes: future months, next iteration, current iteration; however plans are flexible and temporary. A new iteration begins whenever a change is experienced and every time feedback is sought/given from the customer, plans are revisited and revised as part of the planning/feedback cycles.

*

As well as individual, smaller-scale forms of Agile, larger-scale forms of Agile have also emerged to deal with teams on a larger level. These include: SAFe, LeSS, DAD, and Spotify (to name but a few). Each of these has their pros and their cons, depending on the situation at hand. The most popular and most commonly used is SAFe. A recent survey (2021) found that 37% of Agile practitioners use this framework for Agile scaling, due to the multiple ways in which it can be configured and its focus on value streams - which we'll come to look at later.

So, let's have a look at SAFe...

SAFe - SAFe takes the concept of having a single Scrum team and multiplies it so that you have multiple Scrum teams, all working together in what is called an Agile Release Train (ART). Multiple ARTs work together in what is called a Solution Train (ST). Although the model looks very complex, the basis of Scrum remains in place, with a few additional scaled-up elements - such as PI planning (planning across an ART and ST, every quarter). Add in a few other Agile elements - such as Kanban, Lean portfolio management, customer centricity, design thinking, XP, DevOps - and you've got SAFe:

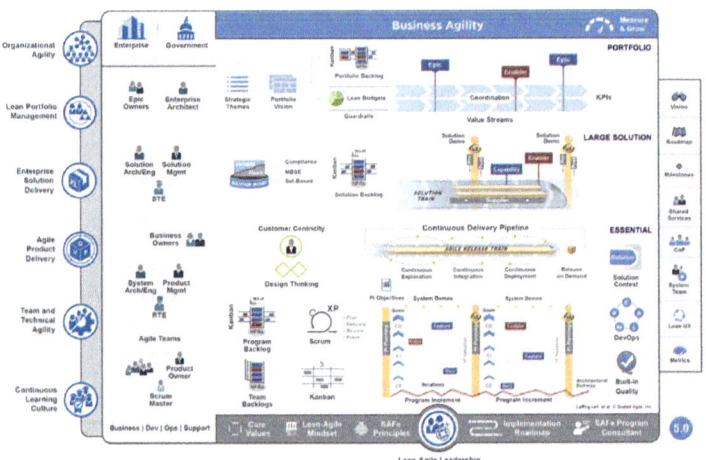

From *https://scaledagileframework.com/*

As mentioned before, SAFe isn't the only way to scale Agile. Scrum at Scale is also another very well-known framework and one of the easiest scaling frameworks to understand, learn and implement.

Scrum@Scale - essentially an extension of Scrum, scaling from one team to a team of teams which orients around core elements such as the Scrum of Scrums (SoS), the SoS master and the chief product owner. It involves a daily SoS meeting, normally taking place after the individual daily stand-ups. The SoS is to bring all the SMs together, aiding communication and coordination among teams and facilitating dependencies or overlaps. It is facilitated by a SoS master (a scaled SM role, similar to the SAFe RTE) and the chief product owner (again, a scaled PO role, similar to the Product Manager in SAFe). It's ideal for an organisation who are already proficient in Scrum and who are looking for a flexible approach to scaling.

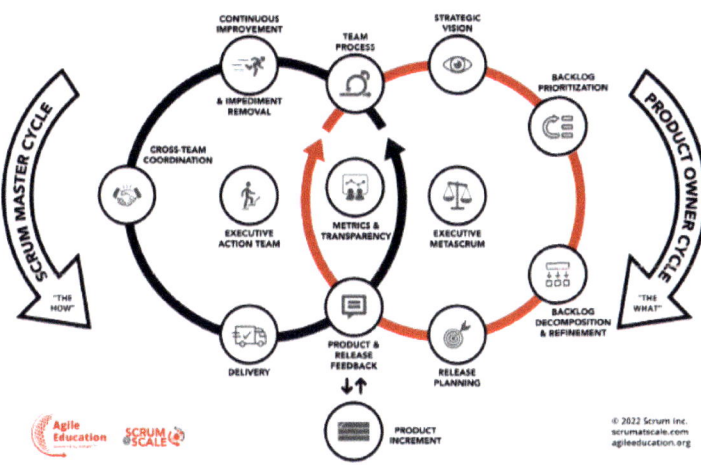

From https://www.scrumatscale.com/scrum-at-scale-guide-online/

LeSS is also another popular framework and is perfect for a startup that is already proficient in Scrum, has limited financial resources and is in need of a lightweight framework.

LeSS - LeSS, or Large Scale Scrum, was forged through over 600 experiments and publicised in a book *Large-Scale Scrum: More with LeSS* by Craig Larman and Bas Vodde. This scaled approach is based around 10 principles:

1. Large Scale Scrum is Scrum.
2. Empirical process control.
3. Transparency.
4. More with less.
5. Whole product focus.
6. Customer-centric.
7. Continuous improvement towards perfection.
8. Systems thinking.
9. Lean thinking.
10. Queuing theory.

Taking these principles, LeSS can be used in either a **basic** configuration - for two to eight teams (10-50 people); or in a **huge** configuration - for more than eight teams (50-6000+ people). With an Area Product Owner, owning the single backlog for the entire of the Scrum teams, LeSS is either approached by taking one requirement area at a time within the larger product, or gradually expanding the entire scope of work of the team, definition of done and the product definition.

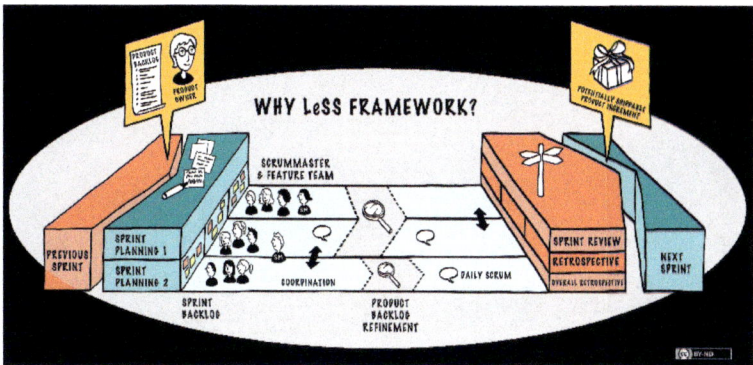

From https://less.works/less/framework

Another popular framework is DAD - Disciplined Agile Delivery. It is different from LeSS or SAFe as it is far more flexible and offers more of a toolbox rather than a framework. It's perfect for a large, well-established enterprise looking for a flexible approach and with financial resources to hire for additional roles, if required.

DAD - Disciplined Agile Delivery was developed in IBM by Scott Amber (2006-2012) and was initially created to complete agile methods - in particular, Scrum - by focusing on how to meet the company's needs for delivery. It merges lots of different Agile methods (Scrum, Kanban, XP), and splits Agile roles into two types: primary roles which are necessary for delivery and secondary roles which are cross-functional, involved from time-to-time. It is characterised by its division of a project into three distinct phases: Inception (launching of the project), Construction (development of the solution), and Transition (delivery).

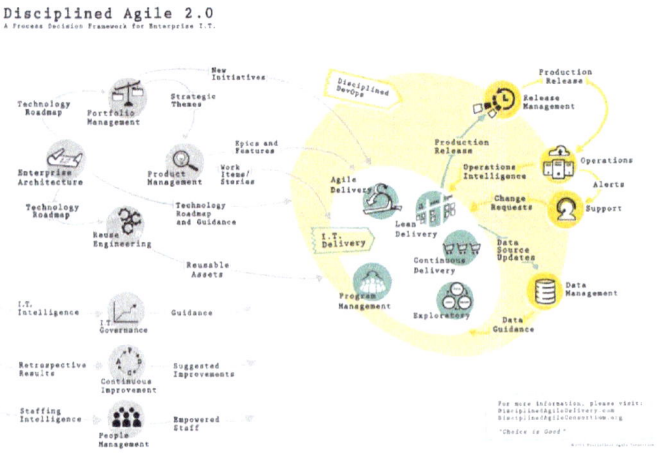

From <https://www.tuleap.org/agility-at-scale/the-top-5-agile-at-scale-methods>

Spotify - as you may have guessed, this model originated with the developers at the well-known music streaming service, *Spotify*. It is very similar to SAFe, with a few key differences:

- Agile teams are called "Squads" and have between 5-10 members. They are multidisciplinary and autonomous.

- Squads are organised into "Tribes", according to the functional/ technical challenges which they face.

- Squad members might be part of a "Chapter" which is led by a coach who is responsible for developing members of their Chapter, helping them to grow in their skills/ professional development.

- Finally, "Guilds" are voluntary groups of individuals who may join to develop or learn something which interests them - similar to a community club.

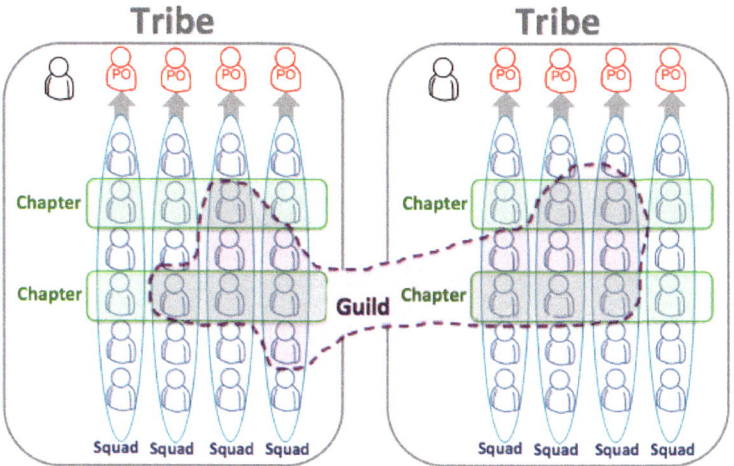

From https://www.agility11.com/blog/2020/6/22/spotify-doesnt-use-the-spotify-model

That's it, in a nutshell: the most common and popularised Agile methodologies and scaled approaches to Agile. As you can see, everyone has a different way of approaching the way that they work but, at the centre of them all is teamwork, collaboration, communication and focus on incremental delivery through regular inspection and adaptation to drive continuous improvement.

Thinking point/ exercise:

Do you work in one of these environments? If so, which one? Does it work for you, or do you think a different approach would be better?

If not, which one do you think would suit your environment? Why?

Let's compare:

Framework	Flexibility	Size	Alignment	Defining characteristics
SAFe	Very prescriptive.	4 different approaches to adoption, offering the ability to flex to your organisational size.	PI planning on regular cadence to enable alignment.	Agile Release Trains and PI planning on cadence to align a huge number of people.
Scrum@Scale	Very elaborate and less flexible to adopt.	5+ teams - unlimited	Forums such as the SoS, SoSoS and MetaScrum offer plenty of opportunities for alignment	SoS and SoSoS - scaled-up versions of DSU for Scrum Masters
LeSS	Your organisation has to change to adopt LeSS as it challenges conventional understanding of projects, products, roles and management practices.	Basic LeSS - 2-8 teams LeSS Huge - 8+ teams	Cross-functional teams	Less artefacts, less process, fewer roles - known for minimal complexity.
DAD	Ability to tailor ways of working to desired approach.	Scaling through self-governance and promotion of enterprise awareness over team awareness.	Goal driven - alignment around delivery of goal/ software.	Promotes risk-value lifecycle.

| Spotify | Prescriptive and complex with multiple possible approaches to configuration of tribes, chapters and guilds (as well as the base-level squad) | Ability to scale as potentially unlimited. | Self-managing with opportunities for alignment. | Additional features such as tribes, guilds and chapters. |

Value:

Value is determined not by the level of the success but by the person measuring the importance and significance of that so-perceived "success".

Value

A lot of the time we measure the output of a process/ product delivery. Take, for example, this user story:

> As a Mother, I want a birthday cake so that my daughter can celebrate her birthday with a birthday cake.

Taken down to the bare bones, this user story requires a cake. This cake could be approached in many different ways: it could use a difficult recipe with hard-to-source ingredients, mixed and cooked slowly at alternating temperatures to get a particular rise; it could be decorated intricately with three types of icing and ornaments made from meringue and delicate hand-made chocolate adornments... At the end of the day, the output is a cake. But what is the outcome?

One outcome would be a technically brilliant cake. Another could be an edible work of art. Or a yummy snack. But where is the value and who determines it?

The answer to all of this is always: the customer determines the value of a product/ process/ experience. They do this by assessing it against some of the following criterion:

- Does it meet my "must have" needs? Is it what I *needed*?
- Is it what I *wanted*?

The true value is found where the need is exceeded and the want is met, and or, exceeded.

So, where does value truly lie? And what is its relationship to the output and/or the outcome?

Let's look back at the user story behind this…

> As a Mother, I want a birthday cake so that my daughter can celebrate her birthday with a birthday cake.

And then answer the following questions:

- Does it meet my "must have" needs? Is it what I *needed*?
    - The mother wanted a cake - it didn't have to be meticulously decorated and ornate and beautiful; nor did it have to be a technically brilliant bake. It just had to be an edible cake, preferably in a flavour that her daughter liked and with ingredients suitable to any dietary needs.
- Is it what I *wanted*?
    - If the mother had received a cake which wasn't suitable for a birthday celebration (i.e. it was too plain or too decorative), or if she had a cake which her daughter didn't like or was allergic to (i.e. it was chocolate and she preferred lemon or it wasn't gluten free as required).

And for the value… Did the daughter have an enjoyable birthday celebration with her cake? That's where the value truly lies: in seeing your daughter happy on her birthday, celebrating with her cake!

Reflect on the following equations:

- **Task + output = outcome (result)**
- **Output + outcome = value**
- **Outcome + value = impact**

How far do you agree/ disagree?

Task + output = outcome (result)

Output + outcome = value

Outcome + value = impact

To summarise:

The outcomes are what the business wants or needs to achieve. The outputs are the actions or items that contribute to achieving an outcome.

Value can be derived from the output (actions/ items) of your work which contribute to the outcome (vision) of the business.

Metric-based value

"What doesn't get measured doesn't get done."

We need to measure our outputs and outcomes, to ensure that we are getting the value that we are aiming for and intend to achieve. Many people try to quantify value in the form of metrics or data. Going back to our original car example, we might determine the value of the car by how fast/slow it can travel; or by how many miles to the gallon it can do; or by how many sales it gets in the first month… All of this is data-based quantifiable value.

When working in an Agile environment, we can also look at our value through use of metrics. These come in the form of charts and graphs, most commonly:

- Burn-down chart
- Burn-up chart
- Velocity graph

So, what do each of these do/ mean? Let's take each of them, separately, and simplify what they are measuring and how we can use them:

Sprint Burndown Chart:

What does it do?

- Records and tracks the workflow of various Scrum teams during agile development in each sprint
- Represents amount of work done during a single sprint / multiple sprints in the form of a graph

How can we use it?

- Compare actual Scrum tasks to estimated Scrum tasks
- Enable insight into Scrum team performance
- Predict more accurately based on previous progress
- Plan workload at the start of sprints more effectively

An Example -

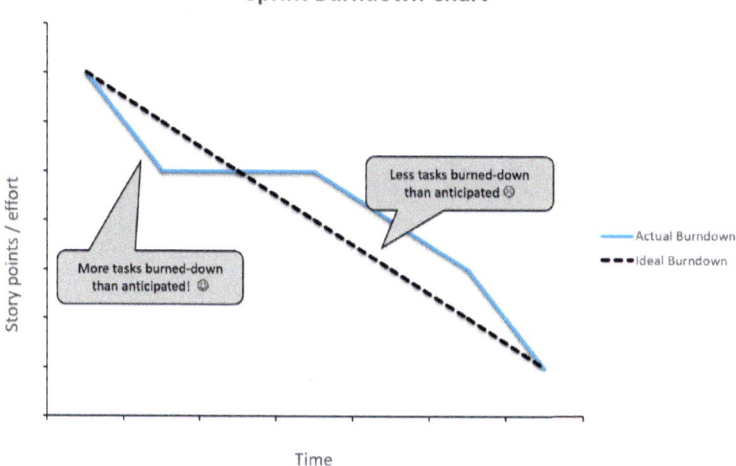

Sprint Burndown Chart

Sprint Burnup Chart:

What does it do?

- Shows how much work has been completed and the total amount of work
- Shows the complete picture of scope – including how it began, where it was added / taken away from, and how progress continued

How can we use it?

- Understand where a project is on / behind schedule
- Understand how much work still needs to be done to meet the deadline

- Demonstrate work completed against scope in a clear single snapshot
- Offer stakeholders reassurance of continual progress

An Example -

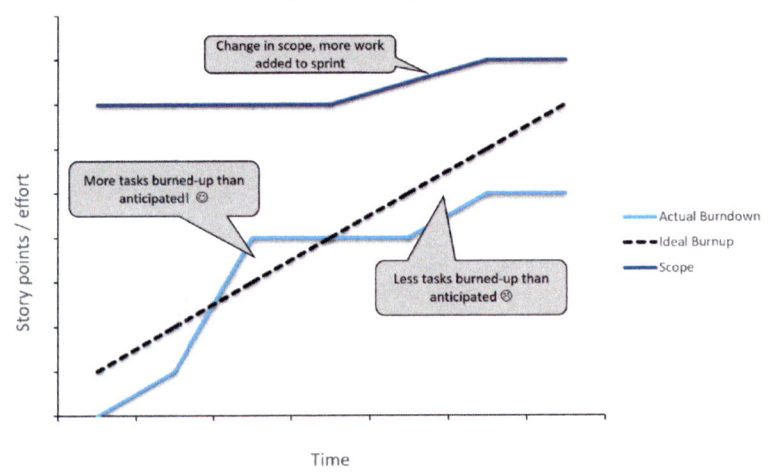

Sprint Burnup Chart

(Chart showing Actual Burndown, Ideal Burnup, and Scope over Time, with annotations: "Change in scope, more work added to sprint", "More tasks burned-up than anticipated! ☺", "Less tasks burned-up than anticipated ☹". Y-axis: Story points / effort. X-axis: Time.)

Agile Velocity Chart:

What does it do?

- Accurately measured the amount of work you want to complete across a specific time frame
- Determines the average workload of an agile project team during a sprint, based on prior sprints and iterations
- Measures the number of story points completed by a team

How can we use it?

- Predict more accurate outcomes of upcoming sprints

- Determined, constant velocity shows team members are moving in the right direction towards project delivery

- Staggering or varying velocity shows team members are struggling with the completion of key project tasks

An Example -

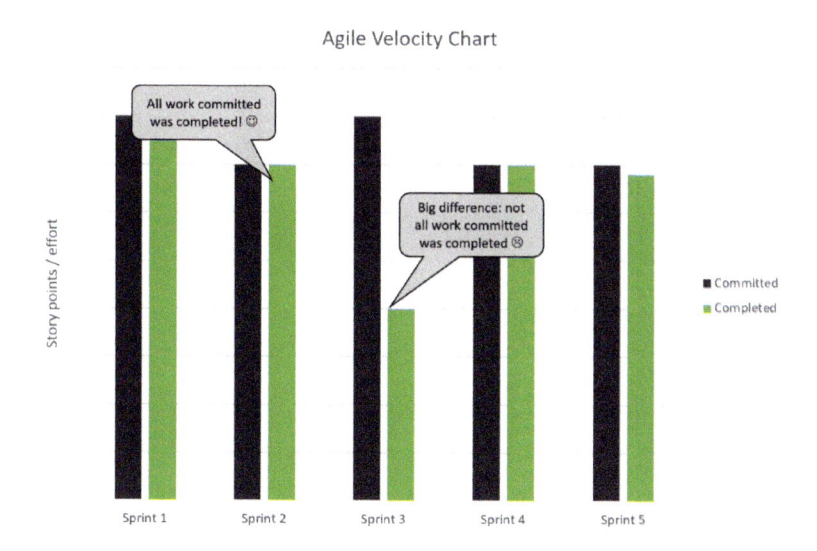

Agile Velocity Chart

These are essentially ways to ensure that we are working at speed, reducing waste and delays, ensuring effectiveness and efficiency, and are working in alignment to achieve the value which we are aiming for.

What do you think you would find helpful? Which of the metrics do you see as most interesting and insightful for a CEO to look at?

Value stream mapping

"A value stream is a step by step process that the organisation takes to deliver value to the end customer."

Essentially, a value stream is a lean manufacturing technique which helps us to analyse, design and manage the workflow so that we can improve the process. It looks at where there are repeated or unnecessary steps (waste) and where we can remove elements which are not adding value (cost and delay).

Value streams map the flow of value from A (the organisation) to B (the customer), taking into account the following:

- **Lead time**: the total amount of time that the entire flow takes, from beginning to end.

- **Processing time**: the total amount of time in each stage (without taking into account time that might be spent waiting/ transitioning between different stages of value creation/ etc).

- **Cycle time:** the average amount of time it takes for each stage in the process to complete.

- **Setup time**: the amount of time needed to prepare/ set up a specific stage/ step in the process.

Let's look at an example:

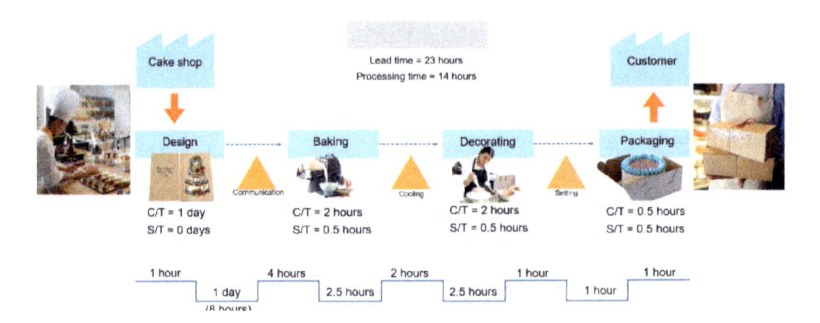

[Diagram: Cake shop value stream example

Lead time = 23 hours
Processing time = 14 hours

Cake shop → Design → Baking → Decorating → Packaging → Customer

Design: C/T = 1 day, S/T = 0 days
Baking: C/T = 2 hours, S/T = 0.5 hours (Communication, Cooling)
Decorating: C/T = 2 hours, S/T = 0.5 hours
Packaging: C/T = 0.5 hours, S/T = 0.5 hours (Setting)

Times between stages: 1 hour, 4 hours, 2 hours, 1 hour, 1 hour
Processing times: 1 day (8 hours), 2.5 hours, 2.5 hours, 1 hour]

Looking at the diagram above, what does this mean?

(Once the customer places the order, it takes an hour to go through to the design team. The design team then takes a full day (8 hours) to design a cake to fit the customer's desires/

requirements. This gets passed to the baking team, which takes 4 hours. The baking team then prepares for half an hour and bake for 2 hours, taking a total of 2 and a half hours to create the cake. This needs to cool for 2 hours before it is ready for the decorating team. The decorating team then takes 2 hours to decorate the cake, with half an hour preparation on top. They then leave it to set for an hour before it is passed to packaging which takes a total of an hour.)

Once you've mapped the value stream of your product/ service, you can start to drive continuous improvement through value stream thinking: a mindset of inspection and adaptation of a process by taking and examining each step in turn.

Taking each step in the process, one at a time, ask yourself the following questions:

- Is this step necessary?
    - If yes, does it add value for the customer?
        - If yes, we keep it as it is a Customer Value Add step.
    - If not, does it contribute to business effectiveness?
        - If yes, we keep it as it is a sustainability step.
        - If not, we identify it as a Non-Value Add step and discuss whether we want/ need to keep it in the process.

What do you see as the advantages/ disadvantages of conducting a value stream mapping exercise? And, what about using the value stream thinking?

(Some, but not all, advantages include: Fewer delays and clearer

ownership; Long-lived, stable teams; Focus on the delivery of value (instead of projects); Faster learning to encourage continuous improvement; Shorter time-to-market / quicker value delivery; Higher quality and increased productivity; Supports Lean mindset development and budgeting – reduction of waste)

Scrum ceremonies:

Scrum that you DO is defined through the Scrum ceremonies.

In Scrum, we have regular ceremonies, scheduled at the same time on the same day in the same place within a regular cadence. This is to reduce complexity and align with the core aim of Agile ways of working: to offer a simple framework for delivery of complex problems within an autonomous working environment.

In Scrum, there are four core ceremonies: the Daily Stand Up (DSU); the Sprint Planning; the Sprint Review; and the Sprint Retrospective. Let's take these each in turn:

The Daily Stand Up:

- What is it? A 15 minute, time-boxed event for daily updates, held at the same time, same place, every day of the Sprint.

- The Purpose: to inspect progress and raise blockers to achievement of the sprint goal and delivery of value.

- The Value: to improve communication, to enable collaboration, and to arrive at completion. In essence, it offers regular opportunities for discussion, identify impediments, promote quick decision-making, inspect and adapt progress towards the sprint goal.

Often, the DSU ends up being a "status report" meeting where individuals just update on their work done/ not done. What is more important: a "status report" or an update on "progress"? How do you differentiate between the two? How do you ensure that focus remains on "progress" (completed/ achieved work as opposed to what you are doing)?

Sprint Planning:

- <u>What is it?</u> The heartbeat of the sprint, the time to plan the work to be done for the sprint ahead and the opportunity to turn ideas into value.

- <u>The Purpose:</u> to plan what can be done, why it adds value, and whether it is a priority for this sprint.

- <u>The Value</u>: to enhance planning, to collaborate on setting a sprint goal, to unite on a vision for the sprint ahead, to offer clarity on the following topics (which are to be discussed during the sprint planning session) :

    - What is this sprint valuable? (and how can we capture this in the sprint goal?)

    - What can be done in this sprint? (what stories are to be selected from the product backlog and how is the PO prioritising these?)

    - How will the chosen work get done? (aligning to the Definition of Done, confirming acceptance criteria of stories, planning capacity of team)

People overcommit when they fail to work within the parameters of their velocity. How can you use empirical thinking to estimate effectively, prioritise, and plan efficiently?

Often, teams end up over-committing during the Sprint Planning session, taking on too many tasks for their upcoming sprint. Why do teams overcommit? Why do you think that this might be an issue and how do you think you can avoid this? Where does velocity fit into this?

Sprint Review:

- <u>What is it?</u> The presentation of work done during the sprint to key stakeholders with opportunity to review and feedback the value from the increment of work created during the sprint. Opportunity to discuss progress towards the product goal.

- The Purpose: to demonstrate an increment and elicit feedback to incorporate others' thoughts, ideas and comments. It enables you to consider these as you determine future iterations and adaptation: an essential part of the inspect-and-adapt cycle of continuous improvement.

- The Value: shared feedback between stakeholders and Scrum team, collaboration on what to do during the next sprint, joint review of progress, inspection and adaptation opportunity.

Sprint Review sessions can become more of a "demo" where the Scrum team shows the work but no feedback is given. What is wrong with this approach and why?

Sprint Retrospective:

- What is it? An opportunity for the Scrum team to come together to inspect the previous sprint, with regards to: individuals, interactions, processes, tools, definition of done, risks and assumptions.

- The Purpose: to improve the quality and effectiveness of the sprint through inspecting the outcome of the sprint. An opportunity to openly discuss and evaluate what went well, what problems arose, and how these problems were/weren't addressed/ resolved. It helps you to go beyond *what* you do and start to examine *how* you do it.

- The Value: shared time for the Scrum team to reflect on their work and ways of working, without the presence of external stakeholders, key parts of inspection and adaptation with attention to the team (not just the increment). This is where quality and effectiveness come into play as you examine how you can improve these.

Sprint Retrospectives can often cause conflict, when members of the Scrum team are honest. Conflict, however, can be managed and is good to address openly. However, what can you do when your Scrum team is not being open in the retrospective? What can you do to create a psychologically safe environment in the meeting to enable team honesty?

Looking at the review and the retrospective, they are both reflective ceremonies: the review looks at what you did whereas the retrospective looks at how you did it. Both, however, are essential to empirical thinking and for driving continuous improvement in delivery of value.

Epics, User Stories, Tasks

Break down the unreasonable into reasonable chunks and suddenly the unmanageable becomes manageable and, before you know it, the unachievable dreams become a reality.

In Scrum, we work with Epics, User Stories and Tasks to enable us to plan out our work. On a scale, the Epic is the 'big' challenge, linked to the vision which guides the team. This Epic consists of multiple User Stories which are smaller activities which contribute to achieving the big challenge. Tasks (an optional additional step) are the singular stages which need to be completed to finish the User Story.

Epics, User Stories and Tasks are written in the same format: As a... I want... so that... The initial "as a" is the actor, the end user who is going to be using the outcome of the user story. The "I want" refers to the action and the person (different to the actor) who will be delivering the user story for the end user. The "so that" refers to the rationale behind the story. IN essence, you are asking yourself three questions: Who are you? What do you want? Why do you want it? (actor + requirement + benefit).

When writing Epics and User Stories, you will have internal and external customers who will be your actors.

Let's look at an example:

> *As a bakery owner, I want cakes baked so that my business remains sustainable.*

This would be the Epic. So what makes up the separate User Stories to enable this Epic to be achieved?

> *As a head baker, I want the necessary ingredients provided for a sponge cake, so that I can use them to bake a cake.*

> Remember: actor = head baker, action = done

by the purchasing team

As a baker, I want the right quantities of my ingredients measured out, so that I can successfully bake a cake.

Remember: actor = baker, action = done by the kitchen team

As a baker, I want a recipe for a simple sponge cake, so that I can understand what is needed and how to bake a cake.

Remember: actor = baker, action = done by the design team

There are multiple possibilities for these User Stories. We could then break down these User Stories into separate Tasks too:

<u>User Story:</u> *As a baker, I want the necessary ingredients for a sponge cake, so that I can use them to bake a cake.*

<u>Possible Tasks:</u> *Research correct ingredients for a sponge cake, Go to the shops, Buy the ingredients...*

What other examples can you think of?

The "Why"?

In order to ensure that we maintain and sustain a systems-thinking culture, we must be able to think and connect and collaborate in different sections and in different fragments of decomposition. A combination of tasks must all align to deliver a story, a combination of stories must align to deliver an epic, a combination of epics must align to deliver a capability... everything must be aligned to an overarching mission, vision and goal. But we can't start out with aiming to achieve the bigger overarching vision, instead we need to break it down and decompose it into smaller chunks, which <u>must</u> be aligned, so that we can deliver iterative and incremental value.

If this is being applied across multiple workstreams, they may have separate tasks and stories however they may share epics. In another example, they may even have separate epics per workstream yet be united by capability. Ultimately they are dependent on each other's delivery of value as they have to collaborate to achieve the overarching vision.

Top tips when writing user stories:

- Remember that if you are the one doing the work, you cannot be the actor in the user story

- If you are the one wanting the work, you cannot be the one doing the work because you cannot inspect your own work objectively

- User stories should always be expressed from the user's perspective - the end user, not the worker (i.e. in the baking example above, the user would be the one buying and eating the cake, not the one making the cake!)

- We must always distinguish and differentiate the actor from the action (the work that is required and the person doing that work)

- Who are you? What do you want? Why do you want it? (actor + requirement + benefit) - three things to ask yourself when writing a user story

Acceptance Criteria, Definition of Ready and Definition of Done

Acceptance Criteria

Once you've written your user story, it is essential that you add acceptance criteria - i.e.: What will be needed to close and complete the user story? What allows the user story to be marked as "complete"?

Examples of acceptance criteria for the stories above could be:

> User Story: As a baker, I want the necessary ingredients for a sponge cake, so that I can use them to bake a cake.
>
> Acceptance Criteria: <u>Given</u> the correct ingredients for a sponge cake and provided in the correct quantities and have been weighed out according to the recipe <u>when</u> the baker has required and requested, <u>then</u> the baker will be able to use them to bake a cake.

As you can see in the example above, we have written the acceptance criteria in the "Given, when, then" format which allows us to have a clear framework to set out the **what**, the **when** and the **outcome**. This is outcome-focussed as well as being specific on the activity to be done, as well as the timeframe. It is essential that the acceptance criteria does not specify the **how**. This is for the individual doing the work to determine.

When writing acceptance criteria, you don't have to use this format. Your acceptance criteria could, alternatively, be written as a list. For example:

> User Story: As a baker, I want the necessary ingredients for a sponge cake, so that I can use them to bake a cake.

Acceptance Criteria: Ingredients for sponge cake identified. Ingredients gathered and measured out in right quantities. Ingredients provided to the baker within timeframes.

In essence, it's up to you in how you want to write your acceptance criteria. However, some key tips to take-away are:

Top tips when writing acceptance criteria:

- Each acceptance criterion should be independently testable.

- Acceptance criteria must have a clear Pass / Fail result so that we can easily determine whether to close the story or not.

- The focus needs to be on the end result, the outcome - the **what** rather than the **how**.

- Include functional as well as non-functional criteria – when relevant.

- Team members should write their own acceptance criteria and the Product Owner/ Scrum Master then reviews and verifies it.

Definition of Ready and Definition of Done

The Definition of Ready (DoR) and Definition of Done (DoD) are key to ensuring transparency and providing quality and value in our final outcome. They are determined by the Scrum team and/or by the organisation as a whole and apply to *all* user stories.

The Definition of Ready states that we have all the resources, knowledge and abilities to start *and complete* the task within the timeframe of a sprint, enabling you to finish your sprint goal. This may take into account basic criteria such as: is it written in the correct format (As a... I want to... So that..); with acceptance criteria and story points? It may also take into account the INVEST approach to writing user stories (see below). You may also decide additional criteria with your team, such as: everyone in the team has to have read and agreed with the story; it must have no external dependencies; it must be sized correctly...

Ultimately, your Definition of Ready is highly customisable to you and your team, but remember that, at the end of the day, all stories must meet this definition of ready before being worked on or taken into a sprint.

Example: As a team, we agree that a story is ready to be taken into a sprint when:

- *it has acceptance criteria*
- *it has story-points, as allocated by the entire team*
- *it has no dependencies*
- *it is written in the correct user story format (as a... I want to... so that...)*
- *it has been approved by the Scrum Master and Product Owner.*

The Definition of Done outlines when a story is ready to be closed and can be marked as "done" / complete, it applies to all of your stories and is not specific to a single story. At the foundation of this is the question of whether or not the story meets its acceptance criteria and has been tested, validated, accepted by the Product Owner and demonstrated and approved by the stakeholders. You may, however, choose to add additional criteria but just remember to make sure that all of your stories are applicable and can meet the Definition of Done as it, like the Definition of Ready, is a universal concept and not specific to an individual user story but applicable across all your user stories and features.

Example: As a team, we agree that a story can be moved to "done" and marked as "complete"/ "closed" when:

- it has met its acceptance criteria
- it has been reviewed and approved by the Product Owner
- it has been demonstrated and approved by the stakeholders
- it provides value to the end-user.

Story pointing and slicing

User stories are all chunks from an epic. When breaking down an epic, we consider various different approaches to taking that large piece of work and chunking it into smaller pieces of work which can be achieved within the space of a sprint. However, we need to be careful that we are splitting our work into small enough pieces so that they do not take up an entire sprint on their own but also so that they are not too small as to not deliver any value independently.

Best practice to remember when splitting up epics and slicing stories is best understood by looking at a cake analogy (again!). When we have a three-layered cake, we may have a vanilla sponge layer, then a red velvet layer and then a chocolate layer. When we eat the cake, we can either eat it layer by layer: vanilla first, then red velvet, and then chocolate; or we can eat it in slices: with a little bit of vanilla *and* a little bit of red velvet *and* a little bit of chocolate. What would you prefer and why?

So, when you're breaking down an epic into stories, and slicing the stories into sprint-sized pieces, what do you think is best: to offer a single, full layer, or an incomplete slice with all the different layers?

Let's put this into practice...

When slicing our epics and stories, we look at different elements. Perhaps these elements are the User Interface, the Back-end, the Testing Platform, Security, Database... If we are slicing horizontally (i.e. like cake *layers*), we would look to deliver all of the Back-end; or all of the User Interface; etc. If we are slicing vertically (i.e. like cake *slices*), we would look to deliver a little bit of the UI, the back-end, the testing platform, security and database all at once in a representative but tiny piece of the whole. This is called an increment.

Once we've decided how to slice our stories, and have made

them the right size for us, so that they can be achieved in a single sprint, we need to add a story point to them. Story pointing is the activity of adding a relative number to a story, offering an estimate for the effort for the completion of the story. This takes into account the complexity of the story, the time it may take to complete, the risks and dependencies associated with completing that story, the amount of work, the uncertainty of any additional factors affecting the story. It is based on the Fibonacci Series (adapted to Scrum), whereby stories are assigned a value from the selection of: 1, 2, 3, 5, 8, 13, 21… as relative to its estimated effort.

How you story point your stories is entirely up to you - whether this is on an individual or team basis. There are pros and cons to both but often, a team approach enables better transparency and accordance on the story and the point assigned. One method, of many, of story pointing as a team is to have a planning poker exercise.

Planning poker is a well-known approach to story pointing where you, as a team, take stories one at a time and discuss the scope, the effort, any risks and dependencies and each decide on a story point for that story. Everyone's individual story point is then shared and, through discussion, you come to a consensus and conclusion on the story point for your story. Repeat with the next story until you've been through your sprint backlog. Simple!

Top tips when story pointing and slicing:

- Agree how you are going to slice your stories: vertically or horizontally - and stay consistent!

- When story pointing, ensure that you consider at least 4 different values (i.e.: 1, 2, 3, 5)

- Ensure the individuals who will be doing the work are included in the story pointing - they have a good view of the effort required as they will be doing it!

- Everyone should give an estimate, even if it's a really rough guess it's valuable to consider

- Set a maximum and minimum story point to the biggest and smallest stories so that you can use this as a starting point for reference

- If a story is too big or significantly bigger than all the others, look to see if you can slice/ split it any more

- Remember there is no wrong or right answer to story points, as long as you agree, and stories/ story points are relative to each other, the story point is valid.

Tools and processes

It is not the tools we use that make us good, but rather how we employ them.

Tools and automation are ways in which we organise ourselves and support our ways of working but ultimately they should not be dictatorial of the way in which we are working. Agile values individuals and interactions over tools and processes, and therefore, although awareness of the different digital tools available to us is important, it should not determine your success in Agile.

Digital tools are always improving, increasing and ever-changing. We'll explore a handful of some of the most common and popular tools currently being used. There are plenty of other options out there but remember, choose the tool to fit the purpose, never fit your purpose/ yourself around the tool!

Monday

- Features - Offers different layouts such as Kanban Timeline or Charts for project tracking, with potential to plan sprints, create user stories, assign to team members, and report on work.
- Pros - Easy collaboration features and 3rd party integration.
- Cons - Less supportive of wider, more complex projects and better suited to smaller teams.

JIRA

- Features - Highly customisable boards and workflows, with out-of-the-box reporting and ability to build dashboards with customisable filters using JQL (Jira Query Language). 1000+ add ons and rich APIs.

- Pros - Very customisable, mature and proven, used by many businesses globally, a range of out-of-the-box features offering potential.

- Cons - Difficult to set up with multiple features and options making it complex, takes time to learn, lots of additional features come at an additional fee.

Asana

- Features - Robust, user-friendly tool with boards, tables, charts and different colours to help you customise your project.

- Pros - User friendly with multiple views available (board, calendar, list) with additional features such as due dates, reminders, prioritisation. Easy integration with a range of programs.

- Cons - Setting up a project can be time-consuming and tricky, the free version is limited and therefore it can be quite pricey.

Trello

- Features - Offers a fun, interactive way to organise projects with to-do lists, user stories, epics and optional add-ons - for example, calendars.

- Pros - Flexible, customisable, intuitive and easy to use.

- Cons - Many features require add-ons, including time-tracking and billing. There is also no option of swim lanes.

Tools are a form of automation, to make the process quicker. They are there to enable and facilitate transparency, inspection and adaptation. Use whichever tool you feel fits your purpose but make sure you use it to your advantage and aren't limited by it.

Roles: a deep dive

Now that we've looked at the tools, methods, processes and artefacts, let's come onto the most important part: the different agile roles. We will be focussing on the role of the Scrum Master, in this book as a whole, however it is important to look at the other roles in your agile Scrum team so that you understand the role and how it relates to you as a Scrum Master.

The **Product Owner** is the value maximiser for the Scrum team. Because they represent the best understanding of the customer needs and desire, they are accountable for maximising the value of the product resulting from the work of the Scrum Team. They are also responsible for managing the Product Backlog effectively. The Product Backlog management includes:

- Developing and explicitly communicating the Product Goal;
- Creating and clearly communicating Product Backlog items;
- Ordering Product Backlog items;
- Ensuring that the Product Backlog is transparent, visible and understood.

The Product Owner may do some of the work in the backlog, or may delegate to members of the Scrum team. Regardless, they remain accountable.

The **Scrum Team members** (or Developers) are the people in the Scrum team who do the work and who are committed to creating any aspect of a usable increment each Sprint. They are accountable for:

- Creating a plan for the Sprint (the Sprint Backlog);

- Instilling quality by adhering to a Definition of Done;
- Adapting their plan each day toward the Sprint Goal;
- Holding each other accountable as professionals;
- Raising any impediments and blockers to their Scrum Master.

Finally, the **Scrum Master** is accountable for establishing Scrum by helping everyone understand Scrum theory and practice. They are also accountable for the Scrum Team's effectiveness. They do this by leading the team and enabling them to improve its practices.

The Scrum Master has many responsibilities to the Scrum team, the PO, the stakeholders, and to the organisation as a whole. These can be understood through looking at the eight stances / "hats" which the Scrum Master must wear. In a nutshell, these are:

- Coach - helping individuals in a limiting mindset to overcome their challenges through offering opportunity to find new perspectives in a limitless mindset.
- Mentor - advising, training and supporting others in imparting knowledge, experience and insight.
- Teacher - instructing, imparting and sharing knowledge to upskill and equip others in Agile knowledge.
- Manager - leading, motivating and supporting the team towards autonomy self-management.
- Facilitator - making a process, event or action easier through enabling and supporting the team in discussions and collaborative communications.
- Change Agent - championing, advocating and promoting change in a healthy and constructive manner so as to

inspire and create lasting change.

- Impediment Remover - responsible for identifying, tracking, and removing impediments which delay or prevent progression.

- Servant Leader - considering the needs of others before your own and leading from behind.

We'll look at these in more detail in later chapters.

Scrum Master as Coach

A coach, similar to a carriage, supports an individual in getting from one place to another, often involving challenging them and taking them from limiting self-beliefs to enabling self-determinism.

The term, coach, came from a slang term used to describe an Oxford University tutor who had 'carried' his student through an exam. The word 'coaching' therefore depicted a process where an individual had helped to transport someone from where they are to where they want to be. As such, coaching as a technique for supporting, training and guiding individuals to self-enablement, was born.

There are many different approaches to how you can coach an individual and multiple models for you to use to guide a coaching conversation to maximise outcome for the individual needing the coaching support.

Let's look at a few:

- GROW: an acronym whereby each letter stands for an element of the conversation: Goal, Reality, Options, Way forward/ Will. This technique helps you guide the conversation through the following questions, moving from looking at the goal (where the coachee wants to be/ what they want to achieve, right the way through to the way forward to achieving that goal):
    - What is your **goal**? What outcome do you want to achieve? Where do you want to be?
    - What is the current **reality**? What is your current situation?

- What **options** do you have that you could take to move forward? What opportunities could you identify to support you to move towards your goal?

- **What** will you do next? Which way forward will you choose?

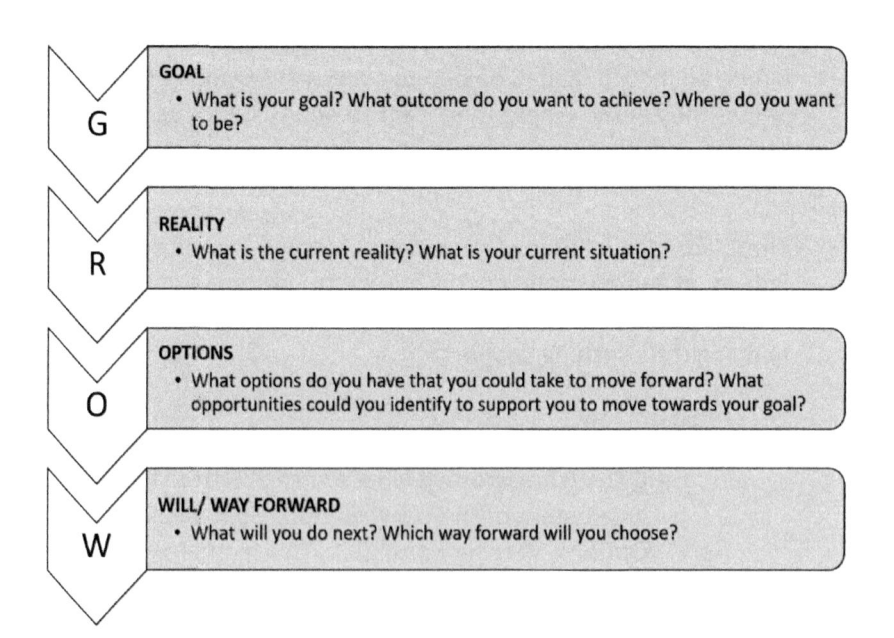

G — **GOAL**
- What is your goal? What outcome do you want to achieve? Where do you want to be?

R — **REALITY**
- What is the current reality? What is your current situation?

O — **OPTIONS**
- What options do you have that you could take to move forward? What opportunities could you identify to support you to move towards your goal?

W — **WILL/ WAY FORWARD**
- What will you do next? Which way forward will you choose?

- OSKAR: another acronym, an alternative to GROW, with slightly different stages: Outcome, Scaling, Know-how, Affirm/ Action, Review. Similar to GROW, it starts with looking at the outcome you want to achieve; then the scale of where you are currently and where you want to be; then the knowledge required to achieve the goal and/or the current knowledge which the individual has; affirming what is going well and action required to improve on this; and then the final review of how it is progressing/ how it went.

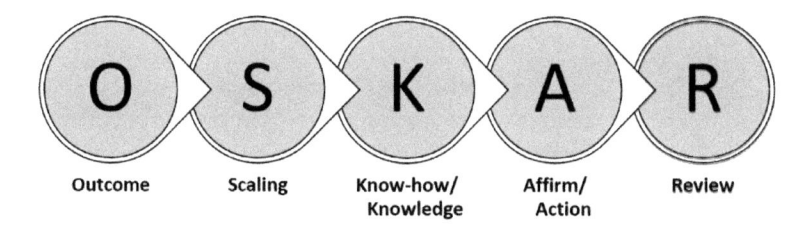

O Outcome **S** Scaling **K** Know-how/ Knowledge **A** Affirm/ Action **R** Review

- FUEL: again, an acronym used to focus the conversation from the current to desired state. This outline looks at Framing the conversation (purpose, goals, desired outcomes); Understanding the current situation; Exploring the desired state; and finally Laying out a success plan.

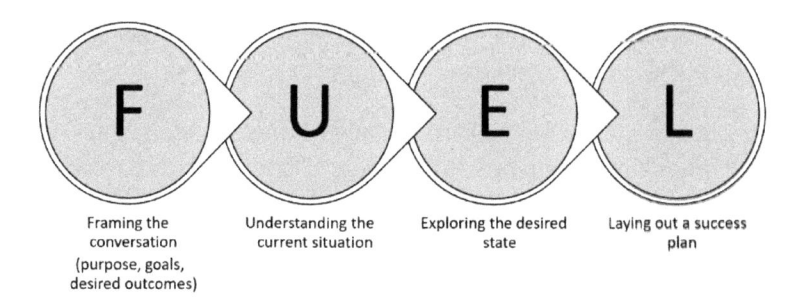

F Framing the conversation (purpose, goals, desired outcomes) **U** Understanding the current situation **E** Exploring the desired state **L** Laying out a success plan

- WOOP: one more acronym to consider, looking at similar elements required to help the coachee get from one place to another by going through the following process: Wish (what the individual wishes to achieve/ accomplish); Outcome (the specifics); Obstacles (considering what could get in their way or prevent them attaining their wish); and Plan (to achieving the wish).

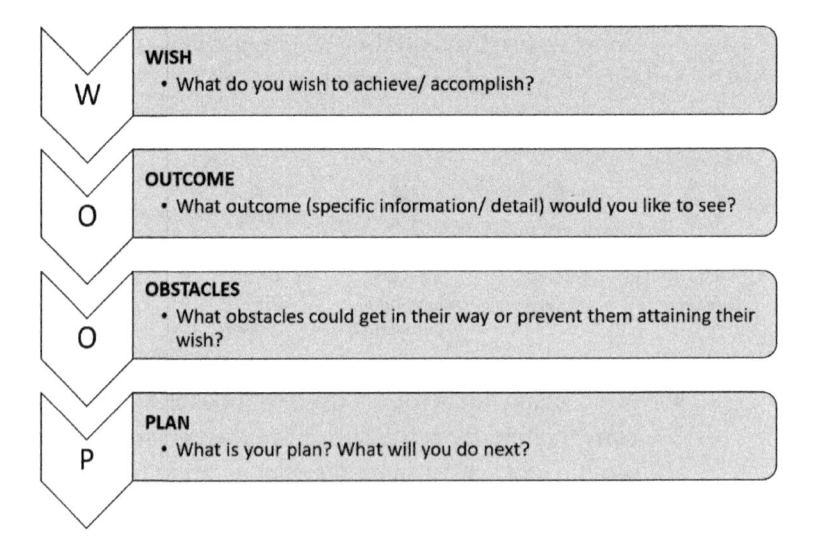

W — **WISH**
- What do you wish to achieve/ accomplish?

O — **OUTCOME**
- What outcome (specific information/ detail) would you like to see?

O — **OBSTACLES**
- What obstacles could get in their way or prevent them attaining their wish?

P — **PLAN**
- What is your plan? What will you do next?

As you can see, there are a plethora of options for you to choose from when framing and guiding your coaching conversation to maximise the benefit your coachee gets and to ensure that you stay on track during your meetings.

Before you start working through any of these models, the coaching relationship needs to be established and, as part of this, you need to consider whether an InsideOut or OutsideIn approach is best. Here's a quick overview of each, with a guide as to when to use each:

- **InsideOut:** An "ask" approach to coaching where the coach focusses on asking the right questions to

challenge the individual to consider different ways of thinking, new perspectives and to ultimately find the answers to their own questions within themselves. This has been proven to be a highly effective form of coaching which has been popularised widely and promoted for its successful outcomes.
- **OutsideIn:** More of a "telling" and "advice giving" approach where the coach points the individual to the answers rather than eliciting the information from them. This approach is best when the coach is an expert who can effectively and clearly communicate their knowledge to a coachee who is desiring to know and learn from them, as well as being competent and driven enough to act on their advice.

In your organisation, you may have Agile coaches - so where does an Agile coach overlap and/or work alongside a Scrum Master?

An Agile coach works with the organisation in more of an "enterprise" role. They are supporting more with the mindset, working strictly with the culture and behaviours to enable Agility across the organisation.

On the other hand, the Scrum Master works within a single team and does not extend beyond the single team - or group. Their remit is on a smaller scale but often still involves the same skill set and activities.

Scrum Master as Mentor

Mentor, originally the name of a friend whom Odysseus (from Homer's Odyssey) entrusted with the education of his son, Telemachus.

There are many different types of mentoring, with the traditional mentoring being more based on one to one discussion however there are other alternative approaches:

- **Group mentoring** - similar to one-to-one mentoring, except including more people. A process where one (or more) mentors provide support to several mentees who often have something in common (for example, they may all be going through an organisational change together). This approach has several benefits: creating a sense of community support, offering multiple perspectives with opportunity for conversation and discussion.
- **Peer mentoring** - a mentoring relationship whether two people are at a similar level/ skill/ experience and provide support to each other. These are often more informal and formed by individuals with joint interests. A great benefit of these relationships is the knowledge sharing that they promote.
- **Reverse mentoring** - it may appear counterintuitive but reverse mentoring is where junior individuals mentor their more senior counterparts. It's a really successful way of breaking down silos, age/ generational gaps/ differences, and can lead to exposure of potential talent to leadership.
- **Flash mentoring** - flash mentoring is exactly what it says on the tin: like a camera flash it is short and over very quickly! This type of mentoring is where the mentor and mentee usually meet for a single, one-off, short session.

They don't require any follow-up and are aimed at tackling a specific issue that can be addressed quickly.
- **Team mentoring** - mentoring a team offers a method for facilitating learning on a team level as individuals go through mutual learning goals and work simultaneously with a mentor (i.e. the Scrum Master) who can support, guide and facilitate their learning.

As a Scrum Master you may encounter a range of these different mentoring types so, to be prepared to mentor in a range of different situations, here are some top tips for approaching mentoring and your mentor/ mentee relationship.

Top tips for approaching mentoring:

- Some people look at the 7Cs of mentorship: Coach the mentee, be a Confidante, provide Career advice, act as a Conduit to others, be a Counsellor to the mentee, offer Critical friendship, inCrease the mentee's visibility and provide them with Choice.
- Practise Active Listening - a key skill in ensuring that you are helping the individual in the best way possible for them. Understand what they need and what they want - not what you think they need or what you think they want!
- Offer support and direction but avoid telling them what to do or which direction to take.
- Give advice but don't make decisions for them.
- Build rapport, trust and a supportive relationship where the mentee feels that they can be open so as to get the most out of the opportunity.
- Have and encourage a growth mindset so as to encourage positive mentality and avoid limiting beliefs.
- Be reflective and consider alternative perspectives.

- Avoid jumping to conclusions, judging quickly or forming fixed opinions.

When mentoring others, in any of the above situations, it is essential that you account for individual and cultural differences. An important part of mentoring and Scrum Mastery is cultural awareness.

The **Culture Wheel** outlines the key elements that are essential to consider when ensuring awareness of other cultures. It takes into account some of the obvious cultural differences such as values, food and drink, the arts, traditions and rituals, language; but also reminds us of the important influences of the different knowledge and stories which other cultures treasure, their different greater community structure and setup, alternative tools and objects or skills and techniques which they may have.

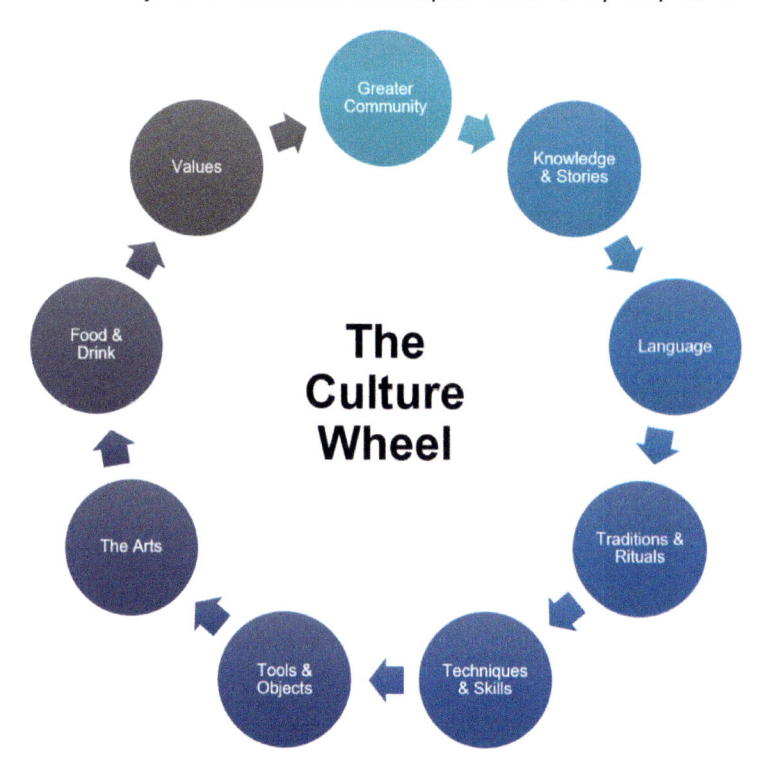

The Culture Wheel

- Greater Community
- Knowledge & Stories
- Language
- Traditions & Rituals
- Techniques & Skills
- Tools & Objects
- The Arts
- Food & Drink
- Values

A lot of these are obvious things which we can see or learn about, however not everything which makes up an individual's culture is evident - seen through their behaviours, attitudes and practices. However, these things are just the tip of the iceberg and are ultimately driven by underlying beliefs, values and perceptions which aren't visible. It is important, when considering individual differences and cultural differences, to look at the things which aren't as visible and hover under the water of the **Cultural Iceberg**:

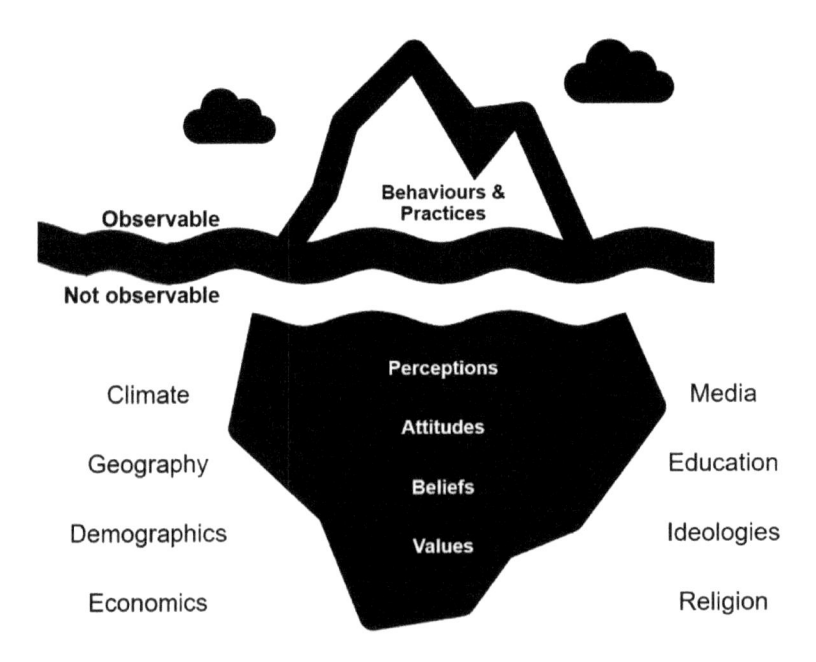

Observable: Behaviours & Practices

Not observable:
- Climate
- Geography
- Demographics
- Economics
- Perceptions
- Attitudes
- Beliefs
- Values
- Media
- Education
- Ideologies
- Religion

Hofstede did research into different cultures and broke down the various differences between cultures into six key dimensions: power distance; uncertainty avoidance; individualism vs collectivism; masculinity vs femininity; short-term vs long-term orientation; and restraint vs indulgence. All of these factors were tested across 50+ countries to offer insight into cultural differences. A break-down of his findings can be looked at, by country, online but here's an overview of what he believes the key dimensions influences cultural differences are:

- **Power distance:** the extent to which an individual/ family/ organisation accepts that power is not distributed equally. Individuals in societies with a high degree of power distance accept hierarchies without need for justification whereas individuals in societies with low power distance seek to have a more equal distribution of power.

- **Uncertainty avoidance**: the extent to which a society will tolerate uncertainty and ambiguity. A high uncertainty avoidance index indicates a society with low tolerance for uncertainty and ambiguity, therefore tending to be more risk averse and more emotional. A low uncertainty avoidance index indicates a society where people are more tolerant of change and often live in an environment with less structure and certainty.

- **Individualism vs Collectivism:** the extent to which a culture is oriented around the individual and their own self-determinism and autonomy or where a culture is focussed on the importance of the community as a whole and their collective goals.

- **Masculinity vs Femininity:** a traditional and ongoing debate around gender stereotypes and how far the culture upholds traditional gender stereotypes or not. For example, a masculine society values courage, strength, competition; whereas a feminine society values cooperation, nurturing and quality of life and love.

- **Short-term vs Long-term Orientation**: this refers to the degree in which a culture prioritises long-term satisfaction and, as such, delays short-term gratification in preference for long-term happiness, or visa-versa. Long-term orientation societies privilege longer-term goals and satisfaction whereas short-term orientation societies place a stronger emphasis on the present rather than the future gratification and happiness.

- **Restraint vs Indulges:** this considers the tendency to restrain or indulge in pleasure. High restraint societies tend to suppress gratification whereas high indulgence societies focus on encouraging a "bon de vivre".

Reflect on some of these cultural elements, as considered in the above models and approaches. What can you see at play in your team? How can that help you to adapt to support the individuals in your team better?

Scrum Master as Teacher

When you teach, you also learn. As a Scrum Master, through teaching others you often also learn more about Scrum and Agile along the way.

Teaching is an age-old approach to transfer of knowledge and goes hand-in-hand with coaching and mentoring however is distinguished by being a more direct approach. It is a more overt process with a clear teacher and learner(s) identified. In your role as a Scrum Master, you will often take on the role of a traditional teacher, instructing in Agile ways of working, teaching what it means to be Agile and how to work in a Scrum environment. This may be on a one-to-one basis but also may involve teaching to the entirety of your Scrum team. As an Agile champion and advocate, you may take on the additional role of teaching your organisation about Agile and Scrum too.

As a teacher, it is important that you are aware of the different ways in which individuals learn. The VAK, or VARK, model is key to understanding the three/ four key ways in which we learn:

- **Visual:** visual learners prefer diagrams, presentations, and images to support their learning.
    - *For example, if you are teaching how the Sprint cycle works, a diagram to show the different artefacts and Scrum events would be useful for a visual learner.*

- **Auditory:** auditory learners learn best through hearing and listening to explanations. Conversation, verbal instruction, or even podcasts would be useful for an auditory learner.
    - *For example, if you are teaching how the Sprint cycle works, a verbal explanation of the different phases and Scrum events, potentially*

accompanied by a podcast, would be best suited for an auditory learner.

- **(Reading & writing):** a newer form of learning which has been added to this model outlines how many individuals prefer to read and/or write things down in order to process, learn and remember them.
    - *For example, if you are teaching how the Sprint cycle works, offering some written material for someone to read, allowing them to take notes while they read, and giving them additional books/ blogs/ information sheets to follow-up with would be helpful for a reader/writer learner.*

- **Kinaesthetic:** kinaesthetic learners prefer to be physically active whilst learning, often enjoying the 'doing' of a task or activity in order to fully understand and internalise learning about it.
    - *For example, if you are teaching how the Sprint cycle works, getting someone to walk around a room as though they are walking around the different sprint events; or actually going through a sprint with them in practice (potentially on a much smaller scale timeframe) would be helpful.*

It is useful when acting the role of the teacher for your Scrum team, it is worth bearing in mind the different ways in which individuals learn so that whether you're teaching on a one-to-one basis or as a group, you incorporate multiple ways of conveying the message so as to appeal to the different learning styles. Another thing to bear in mind is the rationale, the reason, behind your teaching approach - what are you trying to achieve? Ultimately, all learning in Scrum comes down to the

'Scientific Approach', or Empiricism. Remember to hold regular inspection and adaptation events, as well as teaching through clear instruction, so as to guide the team to more natural continuous improvement through their own self-/ and team-inspection process. The most effective way of learning is through experience so, in your role as Scrum master, remember to encompass this in your teaching.

Scrum Master as Manager

Management is a word often branded around too easily, and, similarly are there so many different approaches to management which are mentioned too simply, without real understanding of what they mean and/or what it actually means and entails to be a "manager". Looking back in history, we can see the start of the mention of management back in the 1880s where **Fredrick Taylor** looked at **Scientific Management**: "In the past man was first. In the future the system will be first." In his approach, the managers were elevated whereas the ordinary workers were negated and consequently neglected. This was questioned by **Elon Mayo** in the **Hawthorne Studies** where he looked at additional elements that factored into management - behavioural factors in particular. He concluded that human factors were more important than physical conditions when it came to employee motivation. This approach of looking at human factors for motivation was later popularised by **Maslow's** work in 1954, looking at the Hierarchy of Needs for motivation. Starting with the basic physical needs for food, water, and shelter; Maslow created a pyramid structure to look at the different layers required for motivation, leading all the way up to ultimate self-actualisation and transcendence, when all the human needs were met and the individual felt worthy, motivated and inspired.

1959 saw another take on Maslow's work with **Herzberg's Hygiene and Motivational Factors**, splitting out different factors which contributed to workplace satisfaction and motivation. His theory was more work-place centric and looked at the difference between Hygiene / Dissatisfiers and Motivators / Satisfiers, showing how the base needs of Hygiene were needed before the additional benefits of Motivators were needed to improve employee experience and productivity. **Douglas McGregor** took these two different types of need/benefit and used it to form his model for the two different types of manager: X managers and Y managers. X managers looked at supporting lower-level needs (hygiene factors) in order to coerce and control their employees and workplace; whereas Y managers looked at supporting higher-level needs (motivators) to develop potential in, and inspire their employees. This led to a plethora of additional leadership and management models and styles:

Blanchard and Hersey's Situational Leadership: looking at the situation of the leader rather than the leader as an individual, taking into account the task and the abilities of employees, positioning four different styles of leadership: Directing, Coaching, Supporting and Delegating. Each of these were based around the manager/ leader being either more supportive and cooperative in their leadership style or more directive in their management behaviour. It also took into account the follower's behaviour and how this fed into the leader's consequential leadership approach.

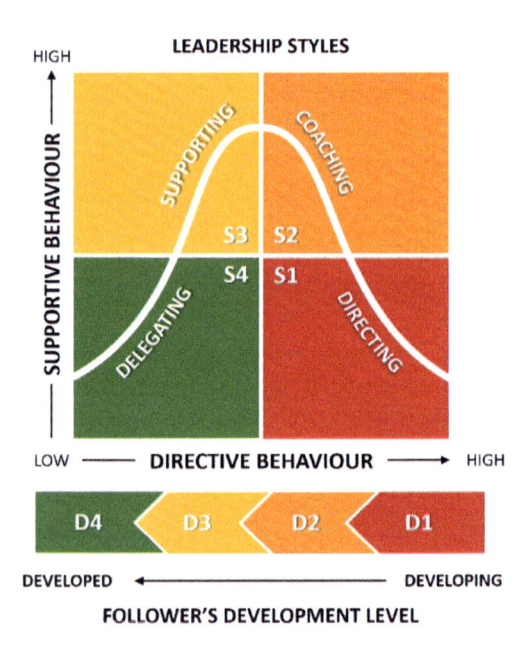

From https://thinkinsights.net/leadership/hersey-blanchard-situational-leadership/

Whichever approach you take to looking at management, the definition of what makes a manager is clear: someone who is responsible for controlling or administering an organisation or group of staff. When looking at Agile, traditional-style managers should not exist; instead, Agile promotes a flat hierarchy. So the Scrum Master, when wearing the "manager" hat should look more towards Daniel Pink for understanding of how to approach management in an Agile environment: through self-determination.

Daniel Pink's theory is all about autonomy and self-determinism in one's approach to not only their work but their day-to-day life. He looks at three elements of work and life which contribute to a stronger sense of self-determination: autonomy, mastery and purpose. Let's break these down:

- Autonomy is about giving individuals the team, time, technique and task; and then allowing them to determine the *how*. This builds their ability to be self-determining and independent in their decision making, action and outcome.

- Mastery focuses on the individual desire to continually improve. If an employee's tasks are too simple or too few in quantity, they experience rust-out and demotivation; if they are too complex or too much in quantity, they experience burn-out and discouragement. It's essential to pair individuals with the right skillset and ability to the right task: challenge them enough yet provide them with enough stability, security and training to motivate them to achieve and progress.

- Finally, purpose. Giving employees clear objectives and intention enables them to unlock the highest level of motivational potential as they strive to contribute to a bigger 'cause' or 'outcome' which demands all their focus and ultimately providing them with an ultimate vision outside of themselves upon which to direct all their attention and determination towards.

Using Pink's motivating factors, how can you manage your Scrum team through motivating them and encouraging them to achieve their own self-mastery and autonomy?

Scrum Master as Impediment Remover

Everyone faces obstacles in life, if everyone had a Scrum Master to remove those obstacles imagine the potential...

A key role of the Scrum Master is as someone to whom any team member can turn to when facing a blocker or impediment. Scrum Masters should act as the point of escalation for any risks or issues, prioritising the removal of the blocker and addressing the risk so as to enable the team member to conduct and continue their work.

Scrum Masters are responsible for identifying, tracking, and removing impediments which delay or prevent progression. The initial part of this - identification and raising of problems - often happens during the Daily Stand-up, or in separate 1:1s with team members. The tracking and escalation can happen through several different methods and forums:

- Scrum Member approaches the team/ individual responsible for causing/ contributing to the blocker or risk

- Scrum Master raises it to the Scrum Master of the team whom they are dependent on and any team who is dependent on them so as to warn of any delays

- Scrum Master raises it to other Scrum Masters/ Product Owners in a wider Scrum of Scrums Ceremony

The Scrum of Scrums (SoS) is a scaled ceremony where all the Scrum Masters get together to discuss issues, risks, impediments and blockers. The aim of the session is to work together to unblock blockers and remove impediments. This session should also enable and encourage transparency around risks and dependencies which teams are facing. It should be a collaborative opportunity to work together to progress as a wider team, by which individual teams are also, consequently, enabled to progress and succeed.

Issues, Impediments, Blockers, Risks…

There's often a lot of jargon and vocabulary around problems so here's a quick reminder and break-down of what each of the following means, how it might be applied. You don't have to use all these but just select a few which work for you and stick to those. Consistency is key in ensuring comprehension and reduction of unnecessary complexity!

- **Risk**: a futuristic problem that *might happen* and which could result in a future impediment/ blocker.

- **Impediment**: a current problem which is slowing progress but not stopping it completely. If unmanaged it could become a permanent problem which results in blocking work and causing it to stop completely.

- **Blocker:** a current problem which has stopped progress completely.

    - **Issue**: a current problem which has stopped progress. An issue is a type of blocker and is currently preventing progress from being made.

    - **Bug**: a system malfunction, an error, flaw, or a default in the system, that causes an incorrect result. A bug is a type of blocker.

Scrum Master as Facilitator

A facilitator is a person or thing which makes a process or action easier, so as a Scrum master, your role is to make the various processes/ events/ actions which involve your team easier. This might be through facilitating conversations around dependencies or blockers/ issues; it may be facilitating workshops or team building sessions to bond the team and get them working more cross-functionally and collaboratively; it may be through facilitating difficult conversations with stakeholders; or it could just be through the daily act of facilitating Scrum ceremonies - the Daily Stand Up, the Retrospective, etc.

Just as we saw and explored the different leadership styles (Blanchard's and Hersey's four styles of: directing, delegating, coaching, supporting), there are also different styles of facilitation and different approaches which can be taken when facilitating a session/ meeting. These correlate to Blanchard's and Hersey's four leadership styles. Different styles may be more/less suited to specific situations and/or certain audiences. In a nutshell, these are:

- Directive: providing information and instruction to develop a plan to achieve the end goal. This correlates to the directing leadership approach.

- Exploratory: asking questions, encouraging people to voice their opinions and share their ideas. This correlates to the coaching leadership style.

- Delegating: assigning tasks to individuals and giving everyone a clear role/ function. This correlates to the delegating leadership style.

- Participative: taking part in discussions, sharing personal experiences and contributing to the session as well as facilitating it. This correlates to the supporting leadership style.

Be mindful of your own personal style as well as what might be better suited to the situation at hand. When you are facilitating, to ensure that your meetings/ sessions are meaningful and valuable, make them POWERful:

- **Purpose** - why is the session necessary? Make sure you know the point of having the meeting/ session. There is no point to having a meeting that has no purpose and does not deliver any value.

- **Outcome-driven** - what are the aimed-for outcomes of the meeting? Where's the value in having this meeting? What do you want to achieve? Meetings that aren't outcome-driven don't lead directly to value; therefore, are they necessary?

- **What's in it for them?** - why should your stakeholders attend? What will they benefit from? What's the value-add for them?

- **Engagement** - how are you going to ensure that everyone is engaged? Sessions without engagement are futile and lack drive, communication, collaboration and consequently, outcome. Engagement is essential to a successful meeting.

- **Roles & Responsibilities** - who does what? Who will facilitate/ attend/ scribe/ etc. Make sure there are clear roles, responsibilities and actions.

P — **PURPOSE**
- What is the purpose?

O — **OUTCOMES**
- What are the aimed-for outcomes of the meeting? Where's the value in having this meeting? What do you want to achieve?

W — **WHAT'S IN IT FOR THEM?**
- Why should your stakeholders attend? What will they benefit from? What's the value-add for them?

E — **ENGAGEMENT**
- How are you going to ensure that everyone is engaged?

R — **ROLES & RELATIONSHIPS**
- Who does what? Who will facilitate/ attend/ scribe/ etc. Make sure there are clear roles, responsibilities and actions.

As well as making your meetings/ sessions POWERful, here are some top tips for successful facilitation:

Top tips when facilitating:

- Stick to the timebox - timeboxing is important. Allocate set parameters of time for different topics/ activities and ensure that you stick to them. This prevents teams going on tangents and supports decision making as well as ensuring the meeting doesn't run over and runs smoothly.
- Clear communication - ensure communication is clear and provide clarifications or support to establish shared understanding of everyone involved to avoid miscommunication or confusion.
- Psychological safety is essential to success - fostering a psychologically safe environment is critical, enabling individuals to speak freely and openly in an environment where there is no judgement, no negativity and where support is offered willingly.
- Active listening - active listening is a skill which everyone should be practising, especially a facilitator!

Look for cues such as body language, tone, eye contact, language used. By modelling active listening, a facilitator can encourage attendees to adopt it too.
- Ask open questions - try to encourage conversation through open questions, and avoid forming any judgement by ensuring your questions are not leading, be objective and neutral.
- Encourage participation from everyone - get everyone involved, make sure everyone has a chance to be heard and contribute to the conversation.
- Establish group rules and expectations - establishing a shared set of rules for engagement and participation can support psychological safety and promote a sense of unity and collaboration as participants come up with, and agree, ways of working together during the session.
- Focus - keep in mind the outcome and purpose of the meeting. Try to avoid taking too many tangents and remember that it's the facilitator's job to keep the team on track by focusing them if they go off-course in conversation.

Another thing to keep in mind is the use of warm-ups, energisers, and games, to engage the team/ individuals in the session you're facilitating. These may not always be appropriate but it is key to remember that people work best when they're working together, bonding together, and most importantly, having fun. Here are a few energiser ideas and games that you could include in your facilitation sessions:

Getting individuals to know each other better - best for team bonding or introductions in a group where others aren't as familiar with each other:

- Two truths and a lie As simple as it sounds, get everyone to come up with two truths and one lie about themselves then go around the room, getting everyone to introduce themselves with their two truths and one lie, followed by guessing what the lie is.

- Human Bingo Everyone has a piece of paper upon which they draw out a three-by-three grid (i.e. with nine boxes) They must fill each of these nine boxes with a statement such as "has brown eyes" / "has children" / "was born in a different country"/ etc (or this grid could be provided by the facilitator). All participants then get up and move around and ask individuals in the group to see if they match the statements on their grid. The person who gets all nine boxes signed first wins.

- Talk about your partner Everyone pairs up and has five minutes to talk to each other and gain as much information about each other as possible. They then have 60 seconds to present back to the group and introduce their partner to everyone else in the room.

- If I was an animal… Go around the room and get everyone to introduce themselves and say what they would be if they were an animal and why they think that they would be like that animal.

- If I was a weather type… Again, similar to the above except with weather types. You can play this game multiple ways and select different metaphors to describe and introduce yourselves.

Energisers to get people working together - perfect for a group who already know/ have met each other, great to get conversation flowing and the team working together:

- Who am I? Pin the name of a different famous person to each participant's back, so that they cannot see it. Then ask participants to walk around the room, asking each other questions about the identity of their famous person. The questions can only be answered by "yes" or "no". First person to guess who they are wins.

- I'm going on holiday! Everyone sits in a circle and the facilitator starts by saying "I'm going on holiday and I'm taking a suitcase..." The next person then repeats and adds what they're taking (e.g. "I'm going on holiday and I'm taking a suitcase and a jumper...") Each person repeats what has been said and adds a new item onto the end of the list and you go round the circle once/twice until everyone has had a turn.

- <u>Height order</u> Get everyone to stand in a line, tallest to shortest, without talking to one another.

- <u>Age order</u> Similar to the above, except with the age from youngest to oldest (again, without talking to one another)

- <u>Alphabet game</u> Starting with the letter A, start a story where each individual says a few sentences and then passes onto the next person in the room, who takes the next letter of the alphabet (e.g. B, C, D...) and continues the story. Example: A long time ago... But then, suddenly... Cats jumped up and... Dogs were barking and... etc.

- <u>Newspaper towers</u> Split the group into teams of 4-6 and give each group a newspaper, a reel of Sellotape and a pair of scissors. They have 20 minutes to construct a tower with these materials. The tower must be self-supporting, stable and must survive a blow test (where someone comes and tries to blow the tower down). The tallest tower wins.

There are so many different games and energisers that you can find and use - here's just a small selection.

Ultimately, facilitation in itself is an art and there are so many different approaches, methods, recommendations that you can look into but it is key to remember what it means to facilitate as a Scrum Master. Similar to your role in removing impediments, your role in facilitation is to enable the team. True facilitation is enablement; whether that's enabling decision making, solution discovery, agreement or clear communication, facilitating a conversation is often the gateway to greater achievement and potential, leading to valuable outcomes.

Scrum Master as Change Agent

Change is the only constant. The world is adapting and so must we, to stay relevant. To stay relevant, we must be Agile.

There are many different ways to approach and manage change and, as a Scrum Master, it is important to be aware of the different models to explain and approach change management. No model is perfect however through understanding the different models, you can take elements from each to be a change champion, advocate and catalyst for change (and Agile) in your Scrum team and in your organisation.

Lewin - Lewin's model proposes that there are three key stages to change, similar to unfreezing and reforming a block of ice: Unfreeze → Change → Refreeze. Each stage is important, with the first stage needing the most emphasis as it enables understanding around why the change is necessary and is essential in getting the buy-in and motivation for the change to be successful.

- Pros - Easy to understand and simple to follow, Lewin model has been used and can be used to implement change and generate momentum needed to create lasting change.

- Cons - Although it is simple to follow, it can be argued to be too simplistic and unreflective of the complexities of change. It is also very rigid, again, failing to take account of the complexities of true change.

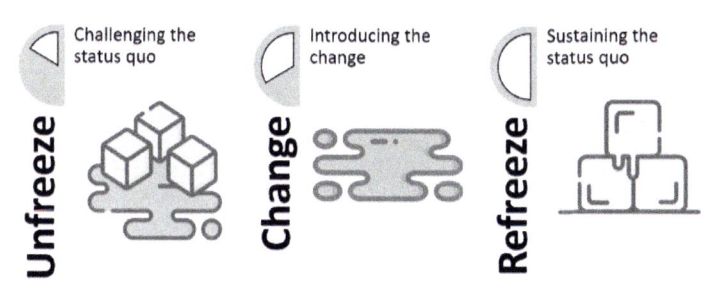

Unfreeze — Challenging the status quo

Change — Introducing the change

Refreeze — Sustaining the status quo

7S Model - McKinsey identified seven internal elements of an organisation that are essential in the change process. The model outlines these elements and promotes their alignment for successful change. These seven elements are: Shared values, Strategy, Systems, Structure, Staff, Skills and Style.

- Pros - This model takes into account both the "soft" and "hard" elements of an organisation, encouraging consideration of many different facets of an organisation when initiating change. These elements can also be useful in consideration of organisation improvement and can feed into a larger SWOT analysis to drive continuous improvement

- Cons - Although the model looks at many different organisational elements, it fails to consider external triggers or factors which could also affect change - e.g: global recession or a pandemic. It is also complex to use and requires a lot of researching and benchmarking.

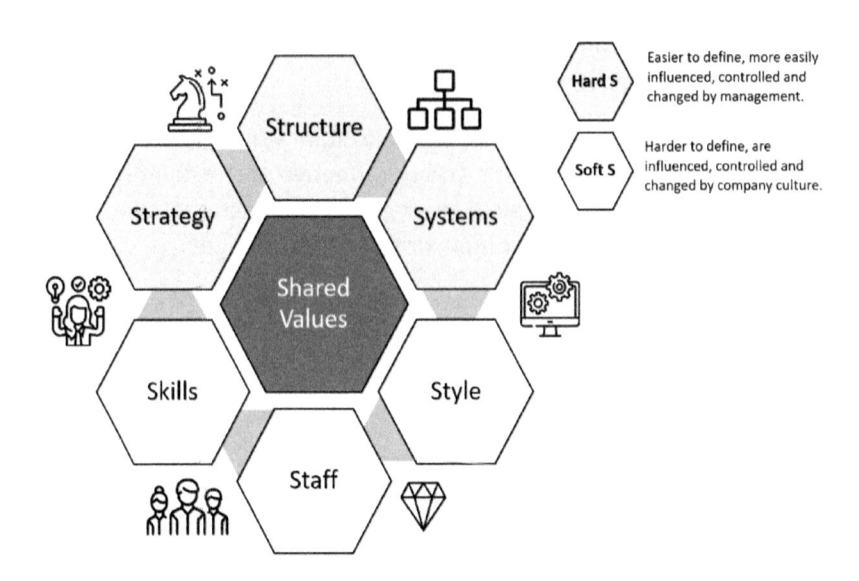

Hard S — Easier to define, more easily influenced, controlled and changed by management.

Soft S — Harder to define, are influenced, controlled and changed by company culture.

ADKAR - ADKAR is an acronym for the five outcomes which an individual needs to be successful in change: Awareness, Desire, Knowledge, Ability, Reinforcement. These can be looked at as separate, consecutive stages in managing a change.

- Pros - This model breaks down the separate stages to change, enabling individuals and organisations to easily track change, goals, development and successes. It also provides a simple framework which is easy to understand, follow and implement.

- Cons - However, ADKAR does not provide micro-level changes or lower-level detail in its model, outlining only a larger-scale picture. It is also less suited to larger-scale change, more useful when looking at incremental change.

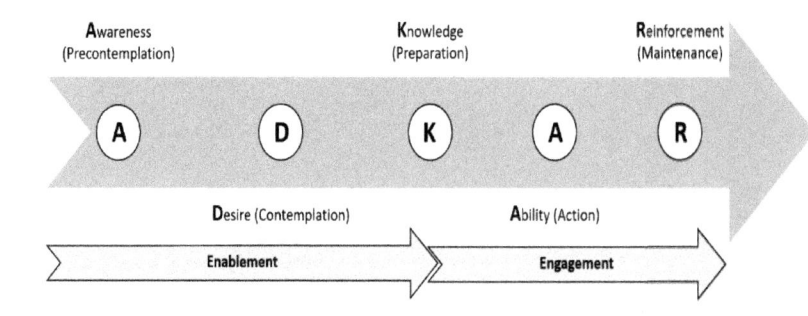

Awareness (Precontemplation) — **D**esire (Contemplation) — **K**nowledge (Preparation) — **A**bility (Action) — **R**einforcement (Maintenance)

Enablement — Engagement

Kotter - Kotter created an eight-step process for how to lead change in an organisation. He listed out eight separate steps to creating lasting change: create a sense of Urgency; build a Guiding Coalition; form a Strategic Vision; enlist a Volunteer Army; enable action by Removing Barriers; generate Short-Term Wins; sustain Acceleration; institute change.

- Pros - Another simple and easy-to-follow model, outlining separate stages which, similar to the ADKAR model, makes it easy to apply and use and track change and progress.

- Cons - It is essentially oriented around top-down change and discourages individual cooperation or input, which can be frustrating for individuals involved in the change.

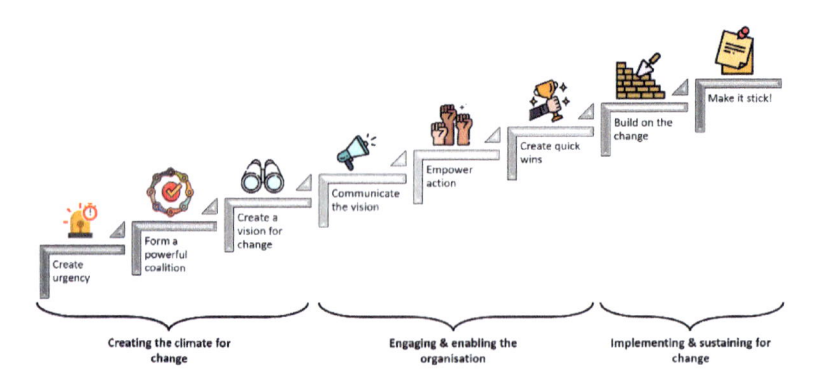

All of these change models look at how you can approach change. The following change model looks at the actual processing of change which an individual/ organisation goes through:

Kubler Ross - Kubler Ross proposed that there were five stages which an individual goes through as the process of change. These are: denial, anger, bargaining, depression and acceptance.

- Pros - It reveals valuable insight into how an individual processes change and how they might feel at different stages of the change.

- Cons - It fails to account for stages happening in parallel or the movement back and forth between stages as its consecutive nature is very rigid and, arguably, unreflective of the complexities of human emotion.

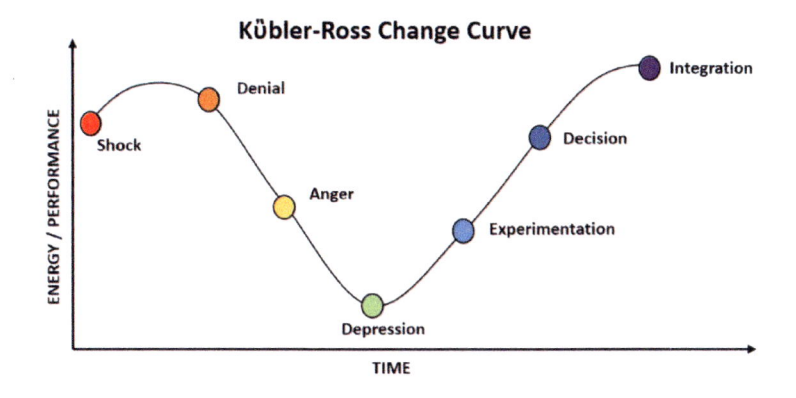

Kübler-Ross Change Curve

A way of looking through all these model to incorporate their various benefits and different perspectives, is to use the **CRIT Model:**

THE C.R.I.T™ MODEL

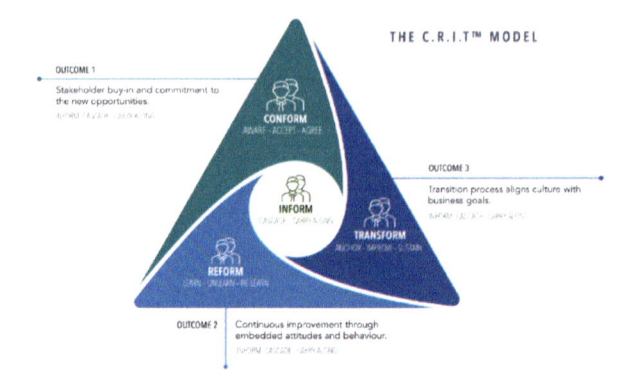

OUTCOME 1
Stakeholder buy-in and commitment to the new opportunities.

CONFORM
AWARE - ACCEPT - AGREE

OUTCOME 3
Transition process aligns culture with business goals.

INFORM

TRANSFORM
ANCHOR - IMPROVE - SUSTAIN

REFORM
LEARN - UNLEARN - RE LEARN

OUTCOME 2
Continuous improvement through embedded attitudes and behaviour.

We use C.R.I.T. as overarching model to facilitate *culture alignment* by:

1. Addressing the employee dissonance that ensues following assimilation and integration of personnel into the new organisation.

2. Identifying and embedding critical learning, unearning, and relearning, to enhance effective assimilation and operation effectiveness following the recruitment and onboarding process.

3. Supporting the alignment of values with a culture that is in harmony with the corporate purpose and organisation goals.

The **TRANSFORM** element is the starting point for the model that enables leaders and decision-makers to align the desired culture with the business goals by mapping out the key objectives and results (OKRs), which is then decomposed, prioritised, and linked to every user story. Hence, achieving strategic alignment in the spirit of systems thinking.

The **CONFORM** element should follow next. In this phase, it is important for the organisation and those involved in the agile initiative, to be clear about the current state of play and the impact it is having on the business – this is the awareness stage. The accept stage allows for deep thinking and clarity of discussion that enables buy-in, by way of identifying and harmonising polarities. This phase is complete when there is, as a minimum requirement, an outline plan for transition to the new state – agree.

The **REFORM** element is the implementation phase of the transition to the new ways of working. It is the journey map that informs and guides the new behaviours that need to be embraced, old behaviours that need to fall away and existing behaviours that need to be done in a different way.

The **INFORM** element is ever present throughout application of the model. It would contain the schedule of activities and initiative that drives effective stakeholder engagement, communication, and collaboration.

Scrum Master as Servant Leader

Coined by Robert Greenleaf in an essay in 1970, Servant Leadership is the act of leading for the greater good, prioritising employee/ team wellbeing and motivation; and empowering individuals to succeed. In this approach, the leader encourages ownership, self-empowerment and autonomy. In teams where the leader serves the team, we can see true team work at play, employee satisfaction and motivation, authenticity and transparency in communications, and autonomy and accountability of work.

Greenleaf further established ten guiding rules of servant leadership. These were:

1. **Listening** - prioritise listening to the team, without interrupting, without asserting your own opinion, without the belief that your opinion is the best/ is "right".
2. **Empathy** - understanding your team members and making the time to get to know them so that you can help to grow them as both individuals and as co-workers.
3. **Healing** - fostering a psychologically safe and healthy environment for team members to work in, giving them the space to heal from any previous negative working experiences, whilst maintaining a healthy work/life balance as well.
4. **Self-awareness** - having a sense of self awareness and insight into your own strengths and weaknesses is essential in any sort of leader, so that you can admit to your vulnerabilities and work on strengthening any areas where you are weaker.
5. **Persuasion** - servant leaders need to be able to persuade and to lead through influence rather than through domination and insistence of power.
6. **Conceptualisation** - having big-picture thinking and a

wider viewpoint whilst planning can help with offering a clear vision for the team.
7. **Foresight** - being able to anticipate and preempt can help leaders to avoid problems and/ or seek out opportunities to improve in advance of disaster.
8. **Stewardship** - leading by example, leading from behind, can help the team to follow suit. Leaders often say but don't often do; being a leader that practises as he preaches is important.
9. **Commitment to people-growth** - empowering team members to grow needs to be extended to the point where you are organising and facilitating learning opportunities, development programmes and coaching.
10. **Building a community** - teams who bond together, grow together and perform better together. Having a sense of community is essential and, as a leader, this is something which is a priority for you.

Building a team

Teamwork has been taught multiple times over, and in a plethora of different approaches and utilising many methods. Below are a few different ways of looking at what teamwork means, how you can build a team and what methods you could apply when working in a team/ promoting teamwork:

Team Building Lessons from Animals

1. **Teamwork makes the dream work** - the cattle egret is often seen perching on cattle or grazing other mammals; they are eating the parasites off their (the cattle/ other mammals) bodies and warn them about oncoming predators. Meanwhile, the cattle/ other mammals also help the egret to eat by shaking up grass and dust to disturb the insects for them to feed on. From this example, we learn how teamwork and communication between different teams can foster success and build stronger relationships.

2. **Rotating leaders** - Canada Geese fly in a V formation when migrating and travelling long distances. If the leader of the V gets tired or sick, another goose takes its place. The rotating leadership highlights the importance of a flexible team, the need to watch out for other team members and delegate appropriately, according to team abilities.
3. **Structure encourages efficiency** - bees live in hives of up to 60,000 bees, each with a specific job that contributes to the overall success of the hive. Bees are often seen as a shining example of animal teamwork and in their structure and self-organisation, we can see how important these things, matched with delegation, are to teamwork and productivity.
4. **Communication is key** - dolphins communicate through multiple ways: vocal calls, echolocation, tail slapping… for them, in the ocean, communication is essential for them to direct, lead and protect each other. Similarly is clear communication crucial for team success.
5. **We're all in this together** - wolves travel together in tightly-knit packs with strict social rankings. This forces them to be expert communicators and their howls don't just enable long-distance communication but also distinguishable, individual and communal communication. This emphasises how important communication, across social ranks and as a form of camaraderie and community-building, is essential.
6. **Learning the ropes** - orcas work together to accomplish things and scientists have noted elder orcas nudging and coaxing younger whales, teaching them different hunting techniques. From these orcas, we can see the value of teaching each other; not just the older teaching the younger but also a sharing of experiences and learnings across the entire time.
7. **Big challenges = big cooperation** - sometimes we challenge ourselves and our team to bigger accomplishments. Lions similarly have the challenge of

catching larger prey animals to feed the entire pride (e.g. buffalos, elephants, wildebeest) They can only achieve this when they work together. Just as the lions capture larger prey when working together, so can humans achieve more when working as a team.
8. **Commitment counts** - ants devote their lives to protecting the queen and the colony - even if it means a fight to the death. If the queen dies, then the entire colony may be extinguished because other female workers do not reproduce. Just as commitment and devotion to the colony is essential for ant survival, so is commitment and devotion important in teamwork.

Team personalities

Dr Meredith Belbin studied teamwork for many years and became famous through his publication of his different team roles. He said that in a team, there are nine different types of team role, nine different types of team player and contributor. These are: shaper, implementer, completer finisher, co-ordinator, team worker, resource investigator, plant, monitor evaluator and specialist. He categorised these into three core categories: action-oriented roles; people-oriented roles; and cerebral roles. Each role had its strengths and weaknesses. No role is better than another role and each role is necessary within a team. Have a look at the table below, summarising the characteristics of each role, and see if you recognise yourself in any of them…

	Role	Characteristics/ strengths	Allowable weaknesses
Action-oriented	*Shaper*	Challenging, dynamic, thrives on pressure, has the courage and drive to tackle obstacles head-on	Prone to provocation and often offends others
	Implementer	Practical, reliable, efficient, turns ideas into actions	Somewhat inflexible and can be closed to new opportunities
	Completer finisher	Polishes and perfects, painstakingly conscientious, pays attention to detail	Inclined to worry unnecessary and less willing to delegate
People-oriented	*Co-ordinator*	Mature, confident, clarifies goals and delegates efficiently and effectively	Could be seen as manipulative and keen to offload own work
	Teamworker	Co-operative, perceptive, enjoys working with others, avoids conflict	Indecisive and avoids conflict
	Resource investigator	Outgoing, enthusiastic, explores opportunities	Over-optimistic, loses interest after initial enthusiasm
Cerebral roles	*Plant*	Creative, imaginative, comes up with lots of ideas	Ignores incidentals, quite often preoccupied
	Monitor evaluator	Judging, strategic, sober, weighs up the pros and cons before making decisions	Lacks drive and ability to inspire others, often seen as critical
	Specialist	Single-minded, dedicated, focussed on specialist knowledge	Dwells on technicalities and often ignores bigger picture

By understanding, firstly, your own team preference, you can look at both the strengths and weaknesses to understand how you can harness your strengths but also how you can work on your weaker areas to improve your ability to work in a team.

> *For example - if you are aware that you are a monitor evaluator, try to think about how you can judge less critically, have a more open mind, and try to inspire others in their work.*

Then, by understanding the preferred/ natural roles of your individual team members, you can coach them in developing themselves and support them in the best way possible.

> *For example - if you notice you have a plant in your team, harness their creativity and enthusiasm for ideas whilst reminding them that they also need to keep focussed and bring their attention back to the situation at hand whenever necessary.*

Dealing with conflict

Conflict is inevitable: in any team, in a family, in friendship groups, in life. Knowing how to handle and approach conflict is a valuable skill, especially in Scrum Mastery. When dealing with conflict, there are different types of conflict management style; we liken these styles to animals:

Sharks - competitive approach to conflict. Sharks use force and competition when faced with conflict. They're very goal-oriented and relationships/ people take a lower priority. They don't hesitate to use aggressive behaviour when addressing conflict and can be autocratic, authoritative, uncooperative, threatening and intimidating due to their need to win.

- Appropriate times to use the Shark style:
    - When conflict involves personal differences that are difficult to change
    - When relationships are not critical

- When others are likely to take advantage of non-competitive behaviour
- When resolution is urgent and decisions are necessary
- When unpopular decisions need to be made and implemented

Owls - collaborative approach to conflict. Owls use a collaborative problem-confronting management style when faced with conflict. They value their goals and relationships and see conflict as problems needing solutions to be found in a way that is agreeable to both sides.

- Appropriate times to use the Owl style:
    - When maintaining relationships is important
    - When time is not a concern
    - When peer conflict is involved and consensus building is important

Turtles - avoiding conflict, turtles try to hide from conflict and withdraw in the face of any conflict. They'd rather ignore it than resolve it, often giving up their own personal goals in order to avoid facing any discord or disagreement.

- Appropriate times to use the Turtle style:
    - When the stakes aren't high or the issue is trivial
    - When confrontation will be difficult and damaging of working relationships
    - When others can effectively resolve the conflict and there is no time constraint

Teddy bears - accommodating and soothing in the face of conflict, teddy bears focus on human relationships and would sacrifice personal goals to preserve harmony and be liked by others. They believe conflict damages relationships and so want to avoid it at all costs. They often give into others' ideas in an attempt to be cooperative, in spite of the fact that it means a loss for them.

- Appropriate times to use the Teddy bear style:
    - When maintaining the relationship is most important
    - When time is limited and harmony/ stability is essential

Foxes - a compromising approach to conflict, foxes are focused on both goals and relationships and try to seek balance. They are willing to sacrifice some of their goals but also for others to give up a bit of theirs too. They are assertive and cooperative in forming a common agreement.

- Appropriate times to use the Fox style:
    - When there are no clear or simple solutions
    - When conflicting people are equal in power and interest
    - When there are no time restraints

Everyone will have their natural tendency towards a certain style, can you spot yours? It is important to be aware of your default approach to conflict but also look at how you can confront conflict in different ways. Also take note of how others approach conflict within your team, what can you see?

Additional Content: Agile Acronyms

User Stories - Good = **INVEST**:
I – independent – can stand alone and deliver value
N – negotiable – open to multiple interpretation
V – valuable – offer value quickly
E - estimable – easy to estimate workload/ time
S – small – bite-sized chunks of work
T – testable – can test to validate easily

User Stories - Bad = **ADAPT**:
A - acceptance criteria – missing or incorrect
D - dependent – dependent on other user stories
A - arbitrary – don't deliver any value
P - perspective – improper perspective
T - too big / too small (too much or too little detail)

What makes a good Sprint Backlog? **DRUM**
- **D**efinition of Done – every item in the backlog must have a predefined, shared set of criteria for its completion, so all team members know when it is done.
- **R**evised regularly – items should be reviewed frequently to ensure commitments can still be met if and when team capacity changes.
- **U**pdated diligently – tasks should be amended and altered to reflect progress of actions and/ or presence of blockers to facilitate cooperation.
- **M**ixture/ variety of tasks – a good sprint backlog should include and address a range of activities to be carried out across all parts of the project/ product (i.e. architecture, coding, testing, UX...)

What makes a good Product Backlog? **DEEP**
- **D**etermined Appropriately – PBIs need to be decided clearly so that they provide clarity on what to do, what needs to be done.
    - Items to be worked on sooner need to be at the top of the backlog and therefore be more detailed. Items to be worked on later will be at the bottom of the backlog and will need less detail.
- **E**mergent – it is a living document, under constant change and iteration as it is groomed and maintained.
- **E**stimated – each item needs a size estimation for the effort required to develop the item.
    - This helps determine the item priority.
    - Smaller, sprint-sized items should be sooner. Bigger items should be later as they need breaking-down.
- **P**rioritised – PBIs should be prioritised. This prioritisation can be changed as you go through and groom the backlog regularly.

Why is the Product Backlog important? **DROPP**
- Provides **DIRECTION** for –
    - Customer/ Client: Customer can see what the next increment/ iteration/ improvement will be. Customers can understand next steps and timeframes. Customers can know what to expect and approximately when it will appear/ be ready.
    - Product Owner: Product Owner can plan and understand when things will be done. PO can shape the overarching project.

- Scrum Master: Scrum Master can see where they are aiming for and guide the team accordingly.
- Scrum Team: Scrum Team can see what they are aiming towards and what they need to do and when they need to do it. The Scrum Team understands where they are going and how they will get there.
- Provides **RATIONALE** – offers a reason behind each of the PBIs as the Scrum team sees how tasks/ user stories support the component.
- Provides **ORGANISATION** – enables items to be arranged according to readiness, priority, need, value, and availability. Re-organisation is also possible, enabling the team to be adaptable, to react to change in an agile way.
- Provides **PERSPECTIVE** – gives the team a sense of what they are aiming to achieve overall, a view of the bigger picture.
- Provides **PRIORITISATION** – enables items to be weighted and ordered accordingly to deliver value quickly. Enables PO/ SM to assign resources to the most important piece of work whilst knowing that other pieces of work will still be completed later.

Mastering Scrum: a Conclusion

To summarise it all in a nutshell Agile relies upon the delivery of value, at speed, without waste or delay, in a customer centric manner. If you are doing Agile, you may be adhering to all the ceremonies and surface-level ways of working; but if you are being Agile, you are embracing the ways of working in a deeper way that models the Agile values, behaviours and principles.

Let's take an analogy… Two children are learning their lessons before taking their GCSE exams. One child does all the past question papers, reads through the revision book, and completes the homework that their teacher sets them, sits and passes the exam. All the information that they learned is then forgotten: they passed the exam so didn't feel the need to remember it. The other child studies all elements that the exam covers, and reads outside the basic syllabus. They research and try to understand additional concepts which can help in their understanding of the basic syllabus. They sit and pass the exam but remember the majority of what they have learned because they have learned it for life. In this example, can you spot who is *doing* the learning and who is *embracing* and *being* the learning?

The same applies to Agile. To truly *be* Agile you need to embrace it, discover additional ways of thinking about it, challenge yourself, question things, and be open to adopting a new mindset and way of working that may be completely different, alien and unnatural to begin with but that eventually enables you to *be* truly Agile.

When looking at our own, and others', understanding and degree of *being* vs *doing* Agile, we can look at CLOMPSE: Collaboration, Leadership engagement, Outcomes, Mindset, Psychological safety, Speed and Events. Through all of these things we can measure the extent to which we, and others, are truly Agile.

Collaboration

- Are you collaborating in an open, transparent and supportive manner?
- Are teams being transparent in the way in which they work together?
- Is everyone aligned in the delivery of outcomes?

Leadership engagement

- Are senior leadership engaged and invested in the delivery of Agile?
- Is Agile understood and is the reason for being Agile understood?
- Are middle-managers being brought on the journey and also advocating Agile ways of working?

Outcomes

- Is the focus on value?
- Are clear value streams in place?
- Is value being delivered in a way that is timely - with maximum speed and minimal waste and delay?

Mindset

- Are the Agile behaviours, principles and values being upheld?
- Are people embracing Agile to the degree where they no longer question it and often instigate and encourage it?
- Are you thinking 'in Agile' or are you thinking 'in Waterfall' and applying the Agile approach on top?

Psychological safety

- Is the working environment safe? Can people be open about their feelings? Is conflict happening in a healthy way?

- Do teams feel empowered to fail fast and improve?
- Are the retrospectives safe spaces to discuss and reflectively inspect our work?

Speed

- Are you delivering at the quickest speed possible?
- Is there any delay or waste in your processes?
- Is value created in an efficient and effective way, using a Lean approach?
- Are blockers and obstacles handled effectively and resolved quickly?
- Are dependencies avoided and/or removed to ensure teams work cooperatively?

Events

- Are events happening on cadence, within the timebox, and are they effective as to their end-goal?
- Are events leading to outcomes?
- Are attendees proactive and attentive during meetings?

We hope that this book has given you both an overview of how to do Scrum but also taught and encouraged you to question how you should do it, how you can do it better, and how you can truly *be* agile - rather than just *do* agile.

MASTERING SCRUM

THE END

MASTERING SCRUM

ISBN: 9798870479248

Printed in Great Britain
by Amazon